TALES FROM
THE HOMESTEAD

Homestead sha[...]
Billy Caswell's
Hooper's kids.

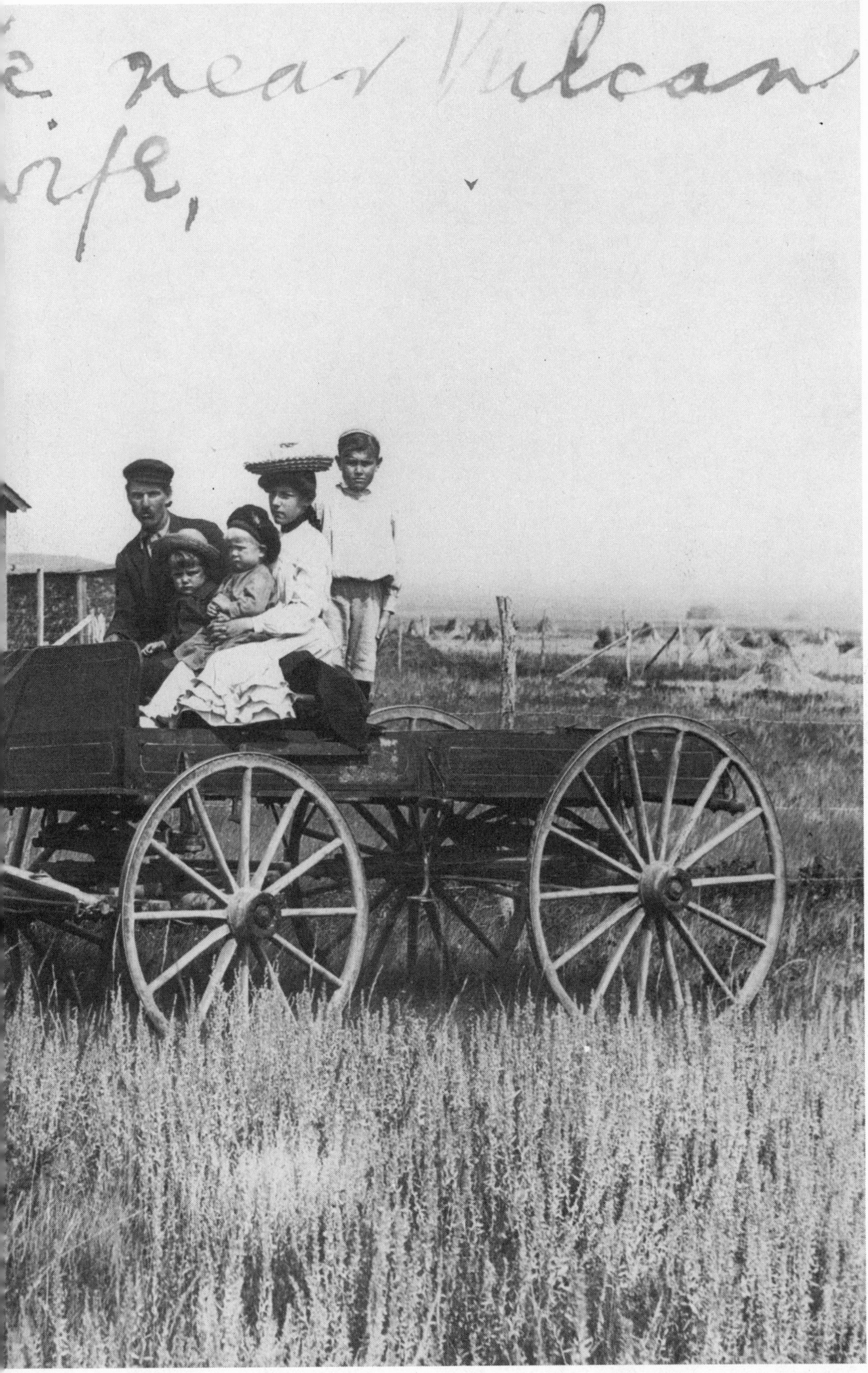
e near Vulcan
ife,

Tales from the Homestead

A History of Prairie Pioneers, 1867–1914

SANDRA ROLLINGS-MAGNUSSON

Heritage House Publishing Company Ltd.
heritagehouse.ca

Cataloguing information available from Library and Archives Canada

978-1-77203-389-2 (paperback)
978-1-77203-390-8 (ebook)

Copyedited by Audrey McClellan
Proofread by Martin Gavin
Cover design by Setareh Ashrafologhalai
Interior design by Colin Parks

Front cover photograph: Image PA-3828-1. Courtesy of Glenbow Archives, Archives and Special Collections, University of Calgary.

Frontispiece: A homesteading family seated on a democrat in front of their A-framed house near Parkland, Alberta, in 1900. *NA-3535-214 by E. Auclair. Courtesy of Glenbow Archives, Archives and Special Collections, University of Calgary.*

The interior of this book was produced on 100% post-consumer recycled paper, processed chlorine free, and printed with vegetable-based inks.

Heritage House gratefully acknowledges that the land on which we live and work is within the traditional territories of the Lkwungen (Esquimalt and Songhees), Malahat, Pacheedaht, Scia'new, T'Sou-ke, and W̱SÁNEĆ (Pauquachin, Tsartlip, Tsawout, Tseycum) Peoples.

We acknowledge the financial support of the Government of Canada through the Canada Book Fund (CBF) and the Canada Council for the Arts, and the Province of British Columbia through the British Columbia Arts Council and the Book Publishing Tax Credit.

Canadá

26 25 24 23 22   1 2 3 4 5

Printed in Canada

The Prairies

These are the gardens of the Desert, these
The unshorn fields, boundless and beautiful,
For which the speech of England has no name—
The Prairies. I behold them for the first,
And my heart swells, while the dilated sight
Takes in the encircling vastness. Lo! they stretch,
In airy undulations, far away,
As if the ocean, in his gentlest swell,
Stood still, with all his rounded billows fixed,
And motionless forever.—Motionless?—
No—they are all unchained again. The clouds
Sweep over with their shadows, and, beneath,
The surface rolls and fluctuates to the eye;
Dark hollows seem to glide along and chase
The sunny ridges.

WILLIAM CULLEN BRYANT
(1794–1788)

Contents

Preface

The homesteading era of 1872 to 1914 was a fascinating period of time. With the implementation of the *Dominion Lands Act* in 1872, men were given the opportunity to apply for entry to 160 acres of homestead land for the price of a ten-dollar registration fee.[1] They then had three years to "prove up" the homestead by erecting a habitable building, breaking ten acres of land in each of the three years, and living on the land for six months of each year. When those requirements were met, the homesteader obtained a patent to the land and was entitled to a pre-emption: that is, he could purchase an additional quarter-section from the federal government, giving him a farm of 320 acres.[2]

This policy provided hundreds of thousands of people the opportunity to improve their lives, as many people, particularly those in Europe, could not foresee a positive future for themselves and their families if they stayed at home. Some were suffering from the effects of a worldwide depression; others were experiencing political and religious purges; and still others faced poverty, unemployment, disease, and starvation. Being offered the chance at a better future compelled many people to grab the opportunity, and, leaving family and friends behind, they travelled by ship, train, and horse and wagon to their final destination—the Canadian western prairies.[3] By 1911, when Canada's fifth census was carried out, 1,162,831 British people (including English, Irish, Welsh and Scottish), 140,022 Germans, 107,757 Austro-Hungarians, 78,458 Scandinavians, and 74,246 French people were living on the western prairies. Those who were Jewish, Dutch, or Russian had approximately 25,000 people each residing in the area.[4]

Along with the Europeans, many Americans also made the trek north to homestead in western Canada. Most of them were already familiar with the homesteading process as they had homesteaded in the Midwestern and western states of the United States under the *Homestead Act* of 1862.[5] By working their land, obtaining their patent, and selling their American homesteads, they had sufficient capital to invest in the free land being offered by the federal government in Canada.

Others migrated to the western prairies from Ontario, Quebec, and the more eastern provinces of the country. These Canadians came from all sectors of society. Some were farm hands, others worked in mercantile and trade shops in local towns or cities, while others laboured long hours in various manufacturing industries. Regardless of where the immigrants or migrants came from, and despite their level of skills in agriculture and animal husbandry, they were all driven by the same motivation—to own land in their own name.

During their journey, many of these immigrants and migrants faced a number of difficulties. For those travelling by ship, the experience was a novel one, but disappointing. Many people found that they could only afford third-class passage and, as such, were placed in steerage, which offered few amenities. Living in close quarters with hundreds of others, enduring seasickness, and sleeping in bunk beds made for an uncomfortable trip of over 4,500 kilometres to the eastern coast of Canada. For those who could afford second-class passage, life aboard the ship was somewhat more agreeable, as the food was more palatable, drinking water was available, and they enjoyed separate rooms; the general day-to-day conditions were also more favourable.

Once they had reached port cities, like Halifax, Nova Scotia, or Montreal, Quebec, the settlers went to the Immigration Halls, where they were checked over by medical authorities to ensure they were not ill with any contagious diseases. Those who were afflicted, or potentially afflicted, were sent to a quarantine station, where they would stay for a few weeks until it was proven that they were healthy.

Those suffering from chronic conditions or unable to financially support themselves were typically returned to their mother countries.[6]

Once deemed acceptable to enter Canada, the settlers obtained their Canadian Pacific Railway (CPR) tickets for the five-day overland trip from the east coast to the prairies. Many stories describe the uncomfortable conditions of the wooden slatted seats on the colonist cars and the back-and-forth motion as the train rode over the rails. Other stories focus on the immigrants' wonderment at the wide-open spaces and abundance of wildlife seen from the rail car windows. Eventually, the settlers arrived in Winnipeg, known as the "Gateway to the West." This was the gathering place where settlers could recuperate and purchase the homesteading supplies that they would need—oxen, horses, wagons, farm implements, building tools, lumber, and grubstakes (that is, enough flour, sugar, oats, coffee, and tea to last a year). Those who needed to work to acquire funds to buy the necessities for homesteading found jobs in Winnipeg or in the surrounding areas.

When the time was right, the settlers and their families either settled in Manitoba or set off on the final leg of their trip into the western reaches of the North-West Territories (which became the provinces of Saskatchewan and Alberta in 1905). Travelling in wagons piled high with their belongings and pulled by oxen or horses, the settlers followed well-established trails and, sometimes, the less-used buffalo trails into the wilds. In small, established towns like Brandon, Minnedosa, Lake Dauphin, Estevan, Regina, Yorkton, Battleford, Prince Albert, Lethbridge, Calgary, Red Deer, Wetaskiwin, and Edmonton, the settlers would visit the local Dominion Lands Office, where they were able to choose a quarter-section from a map and register for their homestead. Once that was done, they would cross the land with their belongings, following the surveyor markers that were found in mounds in the northeast corner of every Section. By keeping track of the numbers on the markers, the homesteaders were able to locate their homestead without too much difficulty.

With the hard work of travelling done, the next challenge was to build a habitable home. Using resources at hand, many homesteaders lived in soddies or log homes when they first arrived, followed by framed houses at a later date. Planting gardens; breaking and cropping fields with wheat, oats, or flax; building barns, sheds, and granaries; and digging wells were important tasks that needed to be accomplished before the freezing temperatures of the winter set in. Women taking care of small children, cooking, and cleaning; men working out-of-doors with stock and ploughing fields; and older children helping out with a variety of chores became everyday undertakings. Hunting small animals and birds, collecting berries, and preserving food also became important aspects of homesteading life, as such jobs helped to ensure the survival of the family.

Even as families became settled into a routine, they were confronted, from time to time, with various dangers that threatened their lives. Aside from the wild animals that lived in the area, like black bears and cougars, some homesteaders battled prairie fires that swept across their fields, destroying and killing everything in the path of the flames. Cyclones were not unheard of, and homes and barns could be demolished and lives taken within seconds as a cyclone passed through. People caught outside in a blizzard or freezing temperatures during the winter months could suffer frostbite or might even freeze to death if they did not find shelter within a short period of time. And if there was a medical emergency, the lack of health facilities, doctors, and nurses on the prairies meant it was not certain the patient would survive.[7]

In short, life was not easy for many of those settlers who came to the western prairies to homestead. This is not to say that there were no pleasant times of solitude or periods of pleasure when one watched the beautiful sunsets, viewed the multitude of prairie flowers in the spring, stood with pride over fields of golden wheat in the fall, or appreciated the wild animals and birds who had made the West their home. Even the freshness of the air was invigorating. Socializing with other homesteaders also became highlights in those early years. Chatting with neighbours, playing games, singing, dancing, celebrating weddings, and attending picnics eased the harshness of prairie life, and these activities were eagerly welcomed by many.

While life was hard, homesteaders relished those years. More often than not, after many years had passed, they remembered both the bad times and the good times, but they also had the satisfaction of knowing that they had helped to develop agriculture on the western prairies. They were proud of their accomplishments and hoped that future generations would remember their efforts. As stated by Charles Kieper in "Keeping the Home Fires Burning," "I would like to leave a little history behind, otherwise some of the doings of the early days will be forgotten."[8]

This book helps us to remember those men, women, and children who had the courage, drive, and perseverance to work the land and build homes across the West. In their later years, some of these homesteaders took the time to put their experiences down on paper. While some stressed the consequences associated with travelling to the prairies, others focused on events that occurred while they built their homes, when they were working with their oxen, cattle, or horses, or when they ploughed, harrowed, seeded, and harvested their fields. For those whose families owned a large number of stock, their stories detail how they rounded up the cattle and branded them and how they protected their herd from wolves. Some stories relate to the injustices endured by the farmers when they went to deliver their wheat seed to the local grain elevators, while others describe the lives of the schoolteachers who came west to teach in the one-room schoolhouses that dotted the prairies.

Each of the stories was written by an individual who resided on the prairies during the homesteading era. Most are first-person accounts, while some wrote their memories in third person. Some of them have been written from the point of view of an adult, while others wrote from a child's perspective. Either way, their memories, informed by the age they were when they came west, offer readers interesting perspectives on homesteading life. We can also readily identify the issues that were important to these people. Their insights, their feelings, and even the words that they use are powerful, as they allow us to step into the homesteaders' shoes and experience life in a different era—a life that is vastly different from the one we have today.

The purpose of this book is to give a voice to those homesteaders who have long since passed away. By bringing together this collection, I hope these stories will be remembered and not forgotten or cast aside. The homesteading era was a unique period of time, one which will never be repeated. As such, it is not only an important part of Canadian history, but is also essential for understanding the heritage and ethnic diversity of the country. I also hope that readers will come to appreciate these homesteading men, women, and children. The obstacles and hardships they had to overcome, and their willingness to work hard and struggle for a better life, offer us insight into their determination to succeed and obtain the title to their land. These dedicated homesteaders toiled endlessly to ensure the prosperity of future generations, and their efforts grant us the ability to recognize the importance of the era and what homesteaders meant to the economic, social, and political development of the three prairie provinces.

EDITORIAL NOTE: With regard to each narrative, it should be noted that some editing changes were required from time to time, all done with the intention of clarifying the points that were stated. Grammatical problems included missing words, spelling mistakes, run-on sentences, punctuation problems, inappropriate verb tenses, and culturally insensitive references. In one memoir, a story delved into one idea that was followed by another, and then returned to finish the original idea. This confusion was clarified by identifying the relevant pieces of the story and placing the pieces together in a coherent fashion. In other cases, memoirs were taken from oral interviews, and editing was done to bring the story together in a meaningful way. When editing changes were made, the author tried to maintain the original vernacular as much as possible so that readers could engage with the stories and gain an understanding of social life and language during the homesteading years.

Tossed into the Scuppers

In the following memoir, Emily Wright Miller recounts her family's decision to move from England to the Canadian prairies in 1903.[1] Her mother, Ellen, had been born and raised in Yorkshire, England, and worked as a weaver when she was a young woman, while her father, Sam, was from the Bradford area of the country and worked as an overseer in a wool-combing mill. Ellen and Sam were married in 1901. Emily remembered how much her father loved the great outdoors and wished for a more pleasant way of life for his family. Her memoir, written in third person, begins with her father returning home from work one day.

■

He was later than usual getting home one evening, and when he did arrive, Ellen knew there was something wrong. He wasn't whistling and he looked tired.

"What's up, Sam? Trouble at the mill?"

Sam dropped heavily into his chair by the fireplace and sighed. "Ellen, I can't take it any longer. I had to speak to one of the workers today. I know he isn't keeping up with the others, but he isn't well. I am very much afraid he is going to lose his job, but what can I do? It's not right."

"You can't do much about it, Sam. It's your job to keep an eye on the others, and you have yourself to think about, you know. It's a good job at the mill."

"Yes, I know that, but I don't like it and I've a mind to quit. I'm fed up with the way things are run."

"What would you do instead?" asked Ellen anxiously.

"I've had an idea in the back of my mind for some time, and the more I think about it the better I like it. But let's have our tea before we talk about it."

When their meal was finished and they were comfortably settled around the fireplace, Sam began, "You know how much I hate pushing people, and you must realize how I hate being cooped up in that noisy mill. A fellow can't get a breath of fresh air all day. However, I've been doing a bit of reading and some inquiring around, and I know where we can have fresh air and space and a good life."

"You mean in the country?" asked Ellen. "You're not a farmer."

"I want to go to Canada. I've been hearing a bit about all the great opportunities there are there. They're begging people to go out and settle in the West. Why, they virtually give a fellow the land just to get people to go and live there." Sam continued, "I can write to the Canadian authorities in London for literature and specific information, and we'll study them first."

Sam wrote and mailed his letter, and finally the day arrived when the postman brought the package of pictures and reading material on Canada. There were brilliant posters and glowing reports of the immensity of that fair land, its healthful climate—hot but invigorating in the summers, and the dry cold of the winters, the kind of cold that didn't penetrate like that of damper climates. Years later, when Sam and Ellen looked back at what they had read, they felt that some of the pictures and statements had been overly optimistic, to put it kindly.

Sam and Ellen pondered over the pros and cons of leaving England and crossing that wide Atlantic Ocean for a new and strange land. Finally, Sam convinced Ellen that it was their golden opportunity. The problem was that those Englishmen who decided to go on this adventure believed that they could make their fortune out there in just a few years, and if things weren't exactly to their liking, they could return to the Old Country. The disillusionment came soon enough, but they were young and eager to see the world outside of their own little England.

The weeks that followed the decision were busy ones. There were visits to relatives before sailing. Packing presented some problems. What would be of the most practical value in their new home? What about their prized wedding gifts? Could they, or should they try to, take them all? They would need warm clothing for the winters and plenty of blankets and quilts. They decided against taking any furniture. The freight might take too much of their money, and they would need every penny to build a house and buy stock and machinery. Sam was quite confident that he could make some of the furniture, and there would be towns where they could purchase a stove and a bed. There was no question about Sam's cello. He couldn't leave that behind. If they had only known what company and consolation that beloved cello would be in the years to come . . . But if they had known what lay ahead, they might never have left England and the comforts they enjoyed.

Ship and train fares varied as to which steamship line and season one chose to travel. Wicker baskets were favourites for packing because they were light and easy to handle, but Sam chose sturdier materials: wood and metal. Money was a consideration, so Sam booked their passage by steerage, perhaps not aware of the poor accommodation it offered. Steerage meant the bottom of the ship, with tiers of open bunks crowded closely together.

Sailing day arrived. It was spring 1903, and the port was Liverpool. They were soon aboard the *Bavarian*, one of the steamships that plied the Atlantic, taking hundreds of pioneers to Halifax on their first leg of the long journey to that wonderful Canadian West.

They made a handsome couple as they stood at the rail. Sam, tall, clear-complexioned with a neatly trimmed moustache, quick to smile and simply but immaculately dressed. Ellen, almost as tall as her husband, tiny-waisted, huge brown eyes, and her auburn hair piled high was a mass of curls. There was nothing now but the wail of the ship's siren as it left the dock. Sam whistled softly as he faced the western sky, but Ellen's gaze lingered on the receding shores of England. She had left everything there—mother, father, sisters, brothers, friends.

Once the boat reached the open Atlantic, there wasn't much time for self-pity. It was cold but not too unpleasant on deck if the day was sunny. There were days when the ocean was rough and the *Bavarian*

⌃ The ss *Bavarian*, an Allan Line ship (identical in appearance to the ship photographed above), was built in 1899 in Scotland. Prior to the 1903 sailing that carried emigrants from Liverpool, England, to Quebec, Canada, the ship had been used to carry thousands of soldiers and officers from England to fight in the Boer War in South Africa. It also made a number of trips returning wounded soldiers and prisoners back to England during the war. In 1905, it was wrecked on Wye Rock, outside of Montreal, Quebec. *Image NA-5394-2 by Jan Wokcicki. Courtesy of Glenbow Archives, Archives and Special Collections, University of Calgary.*

pitched and rolled, causing some to become so ill they wished they had never left home. Sam and Ellen proved to be good sailors, and no doubt the lemons and hard biscuits Ellen's sister had recommended helped prevent the nausea of seasickness—a nausea like no other.

Ellen did have one adventure while on board. She was a hardy individual and had remained in her deck chair despite a very rough sea at one point in the journey. Suddenly, an extra-vigorous roll of the boat tossed her into the scuppers. (This was an opening cut through the waterway and bulwarks of a ship so that water, falling on deck, could flow overboard.) Immediately, two handsome young chaps jumped to her rescue, and by the time Sam appeared, everything was back to normal.

On board, Ellen met other women who were going west, either with their husbands or to marry their sweethearts, who had made the journey earlier. She discovered that they were just as apprehensive as she. They had much in common and were able to bolster each other's courage as they talked of their plans. The time passed quite pleasantly, and Ellen slowly became more cheerful when she knew there would be other women like herself out there on that vast prairie. Little did she realize then that it would be nearly six months before she would have a woman for a neighbour. They were all bachelors.

The passengers had been told that Halifax wasn't too far away, and if they would go to the dining hall, there was a special dinner waiting. That was good news after the poor fare they had been getting, so they lost no time on their way to the table. Just as they were seated and ready to help themselves to the tempting foods, orders came for everyone to line up ready to disembark. Groans of protest went around the table, and one or two were bold and disgusted enough to take with them something that could be eaten on the way. Sam hurried back to get their bags and his precious cello. He had kept it close beside him throughout the voyage, and he didn't intend to trust it to anyone else now.

When everybody was finally lined up, they were so crowded there was scarcely room to breathe. The only way Sam could protect his cello was by holding it by its neck above his head. Then they discovered that they were still some distance from the dock and were obliged to wait for what seemed like hours. When they were able to catch a better glimpse of Halifax, many were surprised to see a city of such size. Some were not well informed beyond the shores of their native England.

The transfer from boat to train proceeded according to schedule. No doubt all were relieved to be on solid ground again. The colonist cars left a great deal to be desired. They were noisy, dirty, and uncomfortable. Anyone who has tried to sleep sitting up for three or four nights will be able to sympathize with these pioneers. The coaches were jammed with immigrants of various nationalities. The combination of body odours, tobacco smoke, and stale air was far more sickening to Ellen than the pitch and roll of the *Bavarian*.

McDERMID
1431

▼ This photograph shows a large number of people waiting at the train station in 1913. *Image NA-1328-1431 by Bryon-May Company Ltd. Courtesy of Glenbow Archives, Archives and Special Collections, University of Calgary.*

Both Ellen and her husband found the toilet facilities distressing. Cleanliness was next to godliness with them. They couldn't have a good wash, a bath was out of the question, and Ellen struggled with her hair as best she could. As the days passed, they found themselves becoming grimy and dishevelled and much in need of a good night's sleep. However, despite the inconveniences they managed to eat, make tea, and doze fitfully.

Some of the passengers had persuaded Sam to play his cello, and a few joined in the singing, led by Ellen's clear soprano voice. Then they begged for a solo. After the last note died away, the applause brought the conductor to the door to see what was going on. He was relieved and happy to find at least one coach of passengers making the best of a long and tedious journey.

For those who had known only the short distances of travel in their homeland, the journey from Halifax to the western prairies must have seemed never-ending. Trees were not in leaf yet, so much of the landscape was bleak—especially those miles, and miles, and miles north of the Great Lakes. Snow was still in evidence there in May.

Somewhere along the journey, several coaches became uncoupled and were left behind. After the fear of having been abandoned had passed, some got off to stretch their legs and get their lungs full of fresh air. It wasn't long before the engineer realized that he had lost part of the train, put his engine into reverse, and picked up the lost coaches.

There were stops along the way, and local women knew that home baking would be a welcome addition to these travellers' meals. As a result, the passengers were able to purchase pies, etc.—the first home baking since they had left home.

Winnipeg was reached at last, but it was cold. As Sam and Ellen were making arrangements for accommodation at the Immigration Hall, a gentleman approached Sam, introduced himself, and told Sam he was an orchestra leader who was looking for musicians. He had, of course, spotted Sam's cello and figured the owner would jump at the chance to join his group. He could hardly believe his ears when Sam told him that he had left one indoor job in the Old Country, and he wasn't interested in taking another. It was going to be a farm for him with space and fresh air.

Were there times in future years that Sam secretly wished he had accepted the offer? If there were, he never let it be known. He maintained until he retired in 1943 that he had never regretted coming to Canada and becoming a farmer on a homestead.

The City Paved with Gold

Like Sam and Ellen, Herman Collingwood and his brother, Allan, also travelled from England to Canada on the Bavarian. *However, Herman, in his memoir, offers a different perspective regarding his and his brother's ocean travels.[1] He also recounts landing in Quebec, riding the rails to Winnipeg, spending some time in the Immigration Hall, and planning for homesteading in Saskatchewan. He offers some political commentary about the* CPR, *which is interesting and highlights reasons for his disdain regarding some aspects of the immigration process.*

■

My father was a farmer in Yorkshire, England, and we were raised on a farm. My brother and I were apprenticed to the carpenter trade and worked five years for board and room to learn the trade and get our papers.

In 1904, the Boer War was just over, and things were very bad in England.[2] So we decided to move out to the colonies. At that time, Canada and Australia were advertising for immigrants, but Prime Minister Wilfrid Laurier of Canada came up with the best offer: 160 acres of good prairie land for ten dollars.[3] You can imagine what that meant to an English boy born on a farm, where a man who owned 160 acres of land was one of the landed gentry. (They forgot to tell us that the government bet you ten dollars you couldn't stay on the land for three years, and if you made it, the land was yours.) The fare from Liverpool to Winnipeg was fifty dollars, meals and tram fare from Quebec to Winnipeg included (third class). Between us, we had enough for the fare and about three hundred dollars to start up in the new world, and, of course, boundless enthusiasm.

On April 28, 1904, we left Father and sister Alice at Paragon Station in Hull, England, with the promise to be back in three years with a fortune. And I haven't seen them since. We offered to bring them out in 1912, but the *Titanic* sank just then and you couldn't get them on a boat for no money. We left Liverpool the next day in the old tramp steamer *Bavarian*. She carried immigrants to Canada, and brought a load of cattle back to England on the return trip. I still believe they treated the cattle better than the immigrants, but, of course, one could get cash for a steer, but an immigrant was just a pain in the neck.

The majority of the passengers were Norwegians, and the balance British. Everything went high, wide, and noisy until we left Ireland and hit the North Atlantic. Then the fun started, and 90 percent of the gang tried to throw up everything they had eaten for the last six months. I held out for two days until I knocked the top off my boiled egg and found that it was as old as ancient Egypt! That finished it. Now I know why they included the grub in the fare: nobody ate.

The cabins were seven feet square, with upper and lower bunks on three sides and the door on the fourth side, and all below the water line. So you can guess we spent most of the time on deck. The grub was dished up in washtubs and you helped yourself. We were lucky. We had six fine boys in our cabin, and we all chipped in and bribed the steward. He got a roast goose or anything we wanted from the first-class pantry. Of course, he stole it, but it tasted OK anyhow, and was a lifesaver after we got our sea legs.

It took twelve days to make the crossing, and I want to tell you, the North Atlantic is no place to be in April. I found the best way of passing the time. I picked up a Scotch girl[4] and joined the rest of the young folks on the afterdeck and watched the sailors checking our speed. One sailor held the watch and the other held the drogue on the line. He threw out the drogue, and as soon as it hit the water, he started counting the knots in the line, and the other counted the minutes. I suppose that is why they give the speed as so many knots. The rest of the time we spent building dreams for the new world. There was no privacy on a boat this size with 2,000 people jammed together, but we got along OK. We were the first ship to make it up the St. Lawrence to Quebec, as the ships stopped off at Halifax during the winter. So we had to push our way through the ice floes. We had something to look at, including seals playing on the ice.

We landed in Quebec and went through customs. A very routine job, as this crowd had very little money and no jewels to smuggle in. Then the doctor checked for the smallpox vaccination mark. Then we hit for the dock to make sure our trunk was safely unloaded. They packed half a dozen trunks together in the hold with a chain around them. The crane and a donkey engine hauled them up and dumped them on the dock. If yours happened to be on the bottom, I hope you had nothing fragile in it. We knew what to expect as my sister had married the chief engineer of a tramp steamer. So we built our trunk accordingly.

On the immigrant train, each car was supplied with a coal and wood stove, which we were supposed to do all our cooking on. The CPR conveniently forgot about the contract to provide board. The two toilets were just two seats with a hole in the floor. The benches were just wood slats without any upholstery of any kind, and we lived, ate, and slept in them for four days, during which time I never had my boots off. After twelve days on a cattle boat in the North Atlantic, this was no hardship. The only time we got a break was when we pulled into a siding in some small town to let a passenger train go by. Then we hit uptown to buy grub, mostly bread and tins of bully beef.[5]

We wondered why we never stopped in any of the cities, but I realize now that this was a CPR project. The government surveyed the western provinces into Townships, Ranges, and Sections. The Townships were numbered north and south, and the Ranges east and west. A Township is a square of 36 Sections, and a Section is one square mile. These are also numbered from 1 to 36. Starting from the lower right-hand corner, or east side, and running 1 to 6 west and 7 to 12 back east, and so on. The government of the day, failing to realize the future value of the western prairies, gave the CPR every odd-numbered Section as an inducement to build the railroad. And worse still, tax free. So half the country between Ontario and British

▾ This was Main Street in Winnipeg, Manitoba, in 1882. *Image NA-118-23 by Steele and Company. Courtesy of Glenbow Archives, Archives and Special Collections, University of Calgary.*

Columbia was owned by the CPR. The only way they could realize anything out of it was to bring in land-hungry suckers from Europe to homestead the even-numbered Sections and build up the country and pay the taxes necessary to develop the country. So the settler started out with a handicap of 50 percent. The Hudson's Bay Company got all of Section 8 and three-quarters of Section 26 out of every Township. All Section 11s were school lands. So we have the reason why the CPR kept us out of the larger towns: we would have jumped the train and stayed there.

So we arrived in Winnipeg, the city paved with gold and the gateway to the promised land. Not the Winnipeg of today, but 1904 in May, with piles of dirty snow still lying here and there in the streets. The winter of 1903/04 was the worst in a decade, but we didn't know that. The station was no larger than the ones you see in the small towns on the prairies. The sidewalks were wood planks and not very even. The streets were paved with wood blocks or just plain mud and no gold. The only large buildings I remember were the Town Hall and the Royal Bank building. There was, of course, no Portage Avenue then, although the city was quite large. We, being above the common herd, registered at the Manor Hotel opposite the station. "Where do we go from here?"

First we were herded into the Immigration Hall to be checked and branded. This Hall was an enormous barn of a building with nothing in it but an office and a bunch of ticks, as they called them—a cotton sack, three feet by six, filled with straw. Not very inviting, perhaps, but free and warm, two very necessary ingredients for a poor immigrant, especially the first.

We contacted the head immigration officer, J. Obed Smith, and when he found out we were full-fledged carpenters with papers to prove it, he shook our hands and told us we were worth our weight in gold out here. The North-West Territories were to be made into the new provinces of Saskatchewan and Alberta the next year, with a thousand towns waiting to be built. So we come to the reason we landed up in the Touchwood Hills district of Saskatchewan. Mr. Smith introduced us to another officer, who had been west with a survey party, and he advised us where to go and why. I always wanted to go south to the open prairie, but Allan was sold on the parklands,[6] where we would have shelter for cattle and water for stock and ducks, partridge, and prairie chicken. Something like home, with cattle, pigs, and chickens—in fact, a real mixed farm. This was the man who steered us to the Touchwood district.

He said, "Your best bet is to follow the new lines building across the Territories. There will be new towns going up every ten miles or so, and there will be a great need for carpenters. The Grand Trunk Railway is just surveying a new main transcontinental line through the Territories in the next three or four years. If you get off the train at Qu'Appelle and go north through Fort Qu'Appelle to Township 26 and take up a homestead, you should be fairly close to the line when it comes through, as I figure it will be about the north end of Township 26."

That man must have had a crystal ball. We settled on Section 34, Township 26, and when the line came through four years later, we were only one and a half miles from town. This man also gave us valuable information as to how to get around in this vast region. From Manitoba to the mountains, 800 miles by 800 miles, with no roads north of the main line, the land was divided into Townships six miles square. This was divided into Sections of one square mile. These were divided into four quarters, half mile square, of 160 acres each. A quarter-section was a homestead, which you got for ten dollars. The Townships were numbered, starting at the US border and running north. Ranges were six-mile-wide columns numbered consecutively from east to west, with thirty Ranges from the First to the Sixth Meridian [from about 97 to 118 degrees west longitude]. So, my homestead was the northeast quarter of Section 34, Township 26, Range 14, west of the Second Meridian. You memorized this and you just couldn't get lost. You'd pull up to a shack anywhere, and even if they didn't know a word of English, you could point to the ground and say "Section," and they could reel off their location, and you would know how to get home. Every Section had an iron stake in the northeast corner with the number stamped on it, and to make it easier to find, they dug four holes, one at each corner, one foot square and one foot deep.

So we decided to spend a few days in Winnipeg, although it wasn't a very appetising sight in May 1904, after a hard winter. You could get a pint of beer at the Tecumpsey [Tecumseh] Hotel for five cents and listen to the stories you could hear in a place like this.

We tried the employment office and found 150 men lined up looking for work. We also found out that the CPR was building branch lines all over the West and were shipping men out to these lines every day. Most of the men took the job to get a free ride as far west as they could get, then jumped the job to spread out all over, so it was a continuous turn.

I think we would have stayed in Winnipeg, but the lure of 160 acres for ten dollars was too strong. And so we moved farther into the unknown, and I began to think that my aunt was right. When we told her where we were going, she said, "The wolves will eat thee up." That is what the Englishmen thought of it in 1904. The Wild West. South-Qu'Appelle, North West Territories. So we arrived at the last stop in our 2,100-mile journey and found our new home.

The Flyer

*In this memoir, Albert Elderton, a young bachelor making his way
to the West to homestead, recalls a devastating railroad accident
where a young man perished.*[1] *He describes the setting of the accident, the actions of the other travellers, and his own sadness at the
realization of how such a hopeful young man, who was going to
begin his life on the western prairies, could lose his life so quickly.*

■

Somewhere in Ontario (the location completely gone from my
memory), our train was sidetracked for quite some time. We were
told to let another train, named "the Flyer" go by. [It was called "the
Flyer" because it would not be stopping at the station but would pro-
ceed at a high rate of speed.]

On one side of the track was a fairly large and level piece of
ground. Having been told by the conductor that we would be waiting for so many minutes until the Flyer went through, most of the
few hundred passengers aboard got off on the inviting level place
to break the tedium of the trip, to stretch their legs, and to smooth
out the wrinkles in certain portions of their anatomy, impressed
upon them by the many hours of reclining on the—shall we say—
none too comfortable corrugated wooden slats of the seats of the
old-fashioned, semi-demi luxurious colonist cars. Be that as it
may, I being possibly of a more or less inquisitive turn of mind

had got off on the opposite side of the car and was poking around among some rocks.

Suddenly, in the distance was heard the warning roar and whistle of the oncoming, thundering "Flyer." For some strange reason, which I have never been able to explain (for I am far from being superstitious), I started to tremble. Some faint intuition or instinct of danger, I suppose. However, I boarded my train and made my way to my seat.

When the whistle sounded, some of the passengers walking around outside hesitated a moment, and then, being new to the country and its ways, perhaps thought [that the Flyer was their train and that the] train would not wait for them to get on and made a rush to the train and dashed up the steps. But a seventy-mile-an-hour Flyer comes mighty fast . . . Jim [Albert's seatmate] said he just managed to grasp the handrail to the steps and hang on for dear life as the mighty, ponderous locomotive and train roared and rattled on its way. He felt a giant suction, pulling at him as he desperately hung on. He turned his head to avoid the flying grit and dust and saw to his horror one of the passengers being thrown over and over, apparently a victim of the vicious suction or else being struck by the flying engine. He watched as our train backed up to bring the baggage car abreast of the body, and the train men lifted him on board. Apparently he had been killed instantly. He was a fine-looking, stalwart lad, and I had frequently seen him. He was noticeable by the fact that he was wearing a brand new suit made out of a new style of cloth then coming into vogue. It was, I believe, a new colour called "olive green." Seeing him then, I often thought to myself, "A new suit for a new life in a new land."

Slowly, our train rolled out of the side track, then stopped at the next station while the body, covered by a blanket, was placed on a baggage truck. We watched as it passed by the window of our car, and the only thing to be seen was a new pair of brown shoes showing at the bottom edge of the blanket. New shoes to tread the new land in the new life, so soon to end in death. How fortunate that many more had not been mangled by that mighty monster in that unthinking dangerous dash. So, somewhat sadly, that sad day our train rolled onward westward to the promised land of the golden West and the boundless prairies and the toils and tribulations of the new life in the new land and surviving. Little dreaming of that time, a little chapter of the poignant homesteading story.

Green Englishmen
Were Not Wanted

William Robinson and his wife decided to make western Canada their home in 1905,[1] after William had spent some time serving with the British Army in the Boer War in South Africa. In this memoir, he recounts some memorable incidents that he and his wife experienced on their travels to the West, particularly being quarantined for a time once they arrived in Canada. William also remembers facing discrimination for being a "green" Englishman and trying to become a homesteader despite his lack of farming skills.

■

My wife, like myself, had no farming experience whatever. She left a comfortable home in the garden of England in one of the oldest towns of that venerable land, the ancient cinque port of Sandwich, Kent, at the age of twenty. We did not know a soul in Canada, yet such is the boundless faith and courage of our women; they left all this to share in the fortunes of the men of their choice.

I was twenty-eight when I arrived in Canada. I had recently returned to England from South Africa, where I had spent three years. We were married in Sandwich on April 20, 1905, had spent about two weeks visiting relatives in England, then sailed from Liverpool early in May, destination Winnipeg and the West we had read so much about. We had a pleasant voyage on the old Allan-line steamship *Kensington*.

When we arrived at the Grosse Island quarantine station in the St. Lawrence River, a suspected case of smallpox was discovered amongst the second-class passengers, so we had to disembark at Grosse Island for a quarantine period of three weeks. Incidentally, the suspect, a young woman, did not have smallpox but some other minor ailment, but anyway, we all had to go ashore at Grosse Island, so that was part of our honeymoon.

This was a great disappointment, of course, but as we were mostly young people, we soon got over it. We had quite comfortable quarters. Each married couple had their own little room, fitted with two comfortable bunks, while single people had their own separate barracks. There was a common dining room and the food was quite good, although, as usual, there was a small number of grumblers. All our clothes and effects were fumigated, and there was one grim reminder of the use of the quarantine station: a monument erected to the memory of four hundred Irish emigrants who had died there as the result of plague and famine.

With the Englishman's love of sport, we soon organized football games and footraces, so the enforcement passed quite quickly and pleasantly. Then we embarked for Montreal, where we were put on colonist cars for Winnipeg. We bought cheap mattresses to make beds out of the hard seats and made our own meals en route. I had a small alcohol stove and had lots of fun. Those colonist cars did not bother me much as I had travelled on worse in South Africa. My wife stood the trip remarkably well with her usual good humour.

We were not much impressed by what we saw of Canada through the coach windows, particularly around the head of Lake Superior. The few shacks we saw along the railway did not seem models of comfort or beauty. There was still some snow around, and the country in general seemed quite forbidding. However, we had come to make a home in Canada and we were not going to be downhearted over trifles.

On arrival in Winnipeg, we secured rooms in a boarding house close to the CPR depot on Martha Street. We then bought some furniture and kitchen utensils, just enough to set up housekeeping. Then

I went to look for work. I was a carpenter by trade, but I was willing to turn my hand to anything. The first place I applied for a job was a new warehouse being built on Main Street just north of the CPR. The foreman, after looking me over, said, "You are an Englishman, aren't you?" I said, "Yes." "Well," he said. "We don't want any green Englishmen here." Well, of course, that gave me a shock as I did not know at that time that there was considerable prejudice against Englishmen in Canada. I did not consider myself particularly green and had probably seen much more of the world than he had. That got me mad and I sure told that boy what I thought of him and his ancestors. As I had seen a spell in the army in South Africa, I had a fairly fluent vocabulary of choice adjectives, and I did not spare any. So my first contact with a Canadian was not very harmonious.

However, I walked on down Main Street and was standing on the corner of Main and Portage when a man came up to me and asked if I wanted work. I replied, "Sure," so he said he could give me a job at two dollars a day moving furniture and files from the old Land Titles Office to the new one. I worked there two days; then I heard carpenters were wanted at the new CPR shops they were building at Weston. Got a job and stayed two years. The pay was thirty-five cents an hour in those days, but I got in a lot of overtime and made out pretty good.

When I left England, I had arranged with my sister's husband and his brother that they were to follow me in 1906 when I had spied out the land, and we would all go farming. My sister's husband was a railway engineer. His brother had done a little farming and market gardening, so he was the farm expert of the crowd. At least, he knew something about farming. As for myself and my sister's husband, we did not know anything. Never been on a farm in our lives.

Unfortunately, our farm expert had only one leg. He had lost the other in a childhood accident, so he was greatly handicapped. In the meantime, in 1905, I had been making inquiries about homestead land, and that is how I met the bricklayer who had a brother, already located in the Ituna district of Saskatchewan, who was an old-timer who had lived and farmed in Manitoba, so I thought his recommendation of land could be relied upon. With our blind selection of land, which, although heavily timbered, was good land, this was another example of how Providence does look after those crazy English.

When my folks arrived in 1906, we talked matters over and decided to locate on the land. So we marched down to the Land Titles Office, where we were shown a large map with many thousands of little squares marked on it showing quarter-sections available for homesteads, and showing also the route of the new transcontinental railway, which passed only five miles from our proposed location. Then each of us paid our ten-dollar filing fee and became potential Canadian landowners.

The in-laws left right away with a certain amount of equipment, chiefly small tools—axes, shovels, picks, etc.—and some money to buy horses and farm implements to start the great adventure. They put up a rude log shelter with a sod roof and a dirt floor. I followed as soon as I got my month's leave from the CPR, my sister remaining with my wife in Winnipeg, where by this time we had rented our own house.

When I arrived on the homestead, things looked pretty tough. The boys had not been used to batching, and the younger brother-in-law, Arthur, was pretty well fed up with conditions. They had no table and used to get their meals, such as they were, seated on the dirt floor with their legs dangling down a hole in the centre, which had been dug to get plaster to chink the logs. I had brought a load of lumber up with me from Balcarres, thirty-five miles away, which at that time was our nearest railway point and stores. So first, I put a floor in the shack and made a table and some benches, and as I proved to be the best cook of the bunch I took over that chore, so things improved quite a bit. The boys had already cut some logs. Then we went to work with a will to build a better house, a storey and a half, as we had room then for both families. Then built a log barn before my leave was up.

We had arranged to pool our resources until we were better able to operate on our own. By this time, we could see we needed additional capital, so I decided to return to my work for the CPR, and my sister rejoined her husband on the farm. I continued to work in Winnipeg until the spring of 1907. Then I, too, left for the farm. We had a little broken on each farm to fulfill the homestead duties.[2]

When I got back to the farm with my wife and our new Canadian baby, I could see we were still short of capital, so I continued to work

▲ People from all walks of life were interested in becoming farmers. In this case, a furniture store owner in England decided to try his hand at homesteading in Alberta. Dated 1912. *Sandra Rollings-Magnusson Collection.*

wherever I could get it until 1910. I built quite a number of log houses and barns for neighbours during the winter. The Grand Trunk Railway came through in 1908, with a village in the making at Ituna. I got lots of work all summer until late fall. Two other Englishmen and myself built nearly all the early buildings in Ituna and back again to the farm, working in Ituna ten hours daily at thirty-five cents per hour.

In 1910, I decided I had either to farm solely or quit and work in the city at my trade, so we decided to split up, and divided our four horses and what little machinery we had. I kept one of my horses for a driver and traded the other one off, bought oxen for my motive power. Now I was really on my own, and many were the dire predictions that I would never make a farmer but should hightail it for the city to work at my trade. But I decided to stick to farming.

Keeping the Home Fires Burning

This memoir was written by Charles Edward Kieper, who was a young boy when his family moved from Germany to the western prairies.[1] What is illuminating about his story is how his family, of limited means, travelled by ship to Halifax, and how they struggled to survive once they reached Winnipeg. Descriptions of how he and his young siblings worked to bring in extra money, his father's experiences with finding work, and his mother's frugalness illustrate the emotional and economic challenges faced by those who had the courage to move to a new country.

We lived in West Prussia, Germany, near Schneidemühl in the village of Tarnow. My mother, whose maiden name was Henrietta Wehr, had been a young widow with one daughter, one year old—Augusta Draheim, born in 1874. My father's name was Johann August Kieper. He had served in the army and fought in the Franco-Prussian War in 1871 and was wounded several times, but not seriously, although he took some scars to his grave. He was a carpenter by trade, for which he served three years as apprentice.

Father and Mother were married in 1875 and lived in the village of Tarnow and farmed a small tract of land near the village. They did not own the land nor anything to work it with, but a neighbour who happened to have time would be hired to do the work. I think they kept some geese, which were used for meat, and the feathers would be used to outfit the beds. Mother used to say there is nothing better than goose feathers in your bed, and that goose fat was a wonderful cure-all. They also kept a few goats, which supplied the milk for the table.

I have often heard Mother and Father talk of how they spent the evenings. They would all go to one another's homes. The girls would take their spinning wheels, as they were doing lots of spinning. Practically all the clothes they wore were homespun and handwoven. The men would also congregate at the same place and spend the evenings playing games. Sometimes the girls would put their spinning wheels in the corner and they would all have a good old dance.

While they lived there, four boys were born to them. Julius was born on March 18, 1876. Albert was born next, but I do not know the year nor the date. I was born on December 23, 1880, and John was born on March 31, 1884. Father and Mother began to think there was not much future in staying there with a family growing up, so they started to dream and began to have visions of a big new country across the ocean.

They made up their minds to sell their few belongings, which was not very much, and follow their dreams. It was quite an undertaking with a family of five, knowing perfectly well that there would be no one there to greet them or give them a warm welcome or handshake or even a friendly smile.

After Father had sold our belongings, he bought our passage to Winnipeg. I remember Mother telling us about neighbours coming in to bid us goodbye, and some women admiring the nice fat cute baby that John was and thought it was a shame to "feed him to the fishes," as they figured he would not stand the trip across the ocean. That was not a very consoling remark. I can imagine Mother shedding many a tear when leaving the country of her birth and her relatives and old-time friends to strike out to a strange country with limited means at our disposal, and no one there to greet us or give us the hand of fellowship. I can't tell the exact date when we left, but it was sometime in May 1884.

I am unable to give any details about our voyage while coming across the ocean. We arrived in Winnipeg on June 18, 1884, and were ushered into an Immigration Hall. It was a long, plain lumber building with sort of stalls along the sides, with some large cookstoves in the centre. We were huddled in one of those stalls with our few belongings piled around us. We cooked our rations on the stoves, which were provided for that purpose. I don't know how long we stayed there.

While we were there, Father went to buy a house or a place to live. He bought a shack on Henry Avenue, not far off Main Street. I don't know how much he paid for it. It was only a very small rough lumber shack, but it was our own home, and we moved into it. I remember Mother telling us that we had eighty dollars left after our shack was paid for. We expected Father would get a job and keep the home fires burning.

Then misfortune stepped in. We all took diphtheria. Albert died before anything could be done. He was buried somewhere in Winnipeg, but I don't think we ever got a trace of the grave. The rest of us were all sick and were taken to the General Hospital. I don't know how long we remained there . . . Anyway, we stayed until we were well. This service did not cost us anything. Our shack had to be fumigated before we could move in.

At that time, Winnipeg was not much of a city. Owing to the gumbo soil, it was very muddy and sticky, and they began to pave Main Street with wooden blocks six or eight inches long, which stood on the ends. That did not make it real smooth, but at least it was a good solid bottom. Otherwise, after a rain, a person could get stuck with a team and wagon right on Main Street. They also put streetcars on some streets. They were pretty small cars drawn by a horse.

Father worked at various places, mostly in the CPR shops or roundhouse, getting from $1.00 to $1.25 per day. In the winter, he would be laid off. One time in the winter, a bunch of men were shipped to Calgary to do some building. Father did not like that kind of building very well. It was not done the way he had learned to do it. They were not particular enough and too much in a hurry.

Mother was keeping the home fires burning, feeding us children and saving every cent she could. She would go to the meat market and buy pig heads because she could buy one for a dollar, which kept us eating for quite a while.

Augusta was working for somebody, looking after children. Julius had made himself a shoeshine box and bought a couple of brushes and went out shining shoes. Those days, there were no shoeshine parlours, but wherever you would find a man with dirty boots and he would consent to have them shined, you would go to work right there and it did not matter where it was, on the street or sidewalk or in hotel lobbies. He also sold papers, so he was able to sell a customer a paper to read while he was getting his shoes shined. I think it was ten cents for a shine. He was doing pretty well at it, as he always was a go-getter. Sometimes, when he could not make a sale of a paper, he would give me a couple and tell me to go and try certain people because they might buy out of sympathy because I was just a pretty small fellow.

The school laws could not have been enforced very much, otherwise Augusta and Julius would have gone to school.

One time when Father was working away from home, I was running around the streets where I had no business and was knocked down by a single horse drawing a light delivery wagon. I don't know whether the horse stepped on my foot or whether the wheel of the wagon ran over it. All I know is that it was good and sore. The man must have been one of those hit-and-run drivers, because he never stopped. I lay there howling my head off because of the pain in my leg, and then a good Samaritan came along who was carrying a bundle of rhubarb on his arm, and he had compassion for me and picked me up. I don't remember what all took place, but I ended up at the police station. In the meantime, it was getting dark, and Mother thought I was with Julius, but when he came home without me, she became alarmed. We had made some friends and neighbours by this time, so she sought the advice of one. He suggested inquiring at the police station. So he and Julius came there, and was I ever glad. The man carried me home and there was great rejoicing over me. But my ankle was still good and sore. Next morning, Mother carried me to the hospital, where they discovered that the little bone in the leg near the ankle was broken. They set it and put it in a plaster of Paris cast and sent me home. Mother used to take me back at different intervals so the doctor could check to see that everything was coming along fine. Anyway, I got over it and was as good as new again.

Things went on in a sort of routine fashion. Father tried to make all the money he could, and that was not too much. Mother saved everything she possibly could and yet kept us clothed and fed. None of us ever went hungry.

We made quite a few friends while we lived there. I will specially mention Mr. and Mrs. Welke, who had a family of two boys a little older than Julius. My father and Mr. Welke would visit together and talk over their problems, and they would talk about the free homesteads that they could get. They finally got in touch with D.W. Riedel, who was working for the federal government. It was his job to try and get German settlers located on the land at Langenburg, at the time in the North-West Territories [later to become the province of Saskatchewan]. Sometime in August 1886, the men got land fever and thought they would follow Mr. Riedel's advice and take up land at Langenburg. Each had saved sufficient money while they lived in Winnipeg to buy the necessary equipment to outfit a homesteader.

The men each bought a yoke of oxen and harness, a cow, a wagon and box, a combination walking plough, four sections of harrows, a logging chain, some chickens, a dog and cat, and a grubstake. Father and Mr. Welke then ordered a railway car and loaded all their belongings into it and billed it out to Birtle, Manitoba—that was as far as the steel was laid at that time. We all got on the train and were certainly thrilled to think we were going to our own farm of 160 acres on the western prairies.

Life Here Was Not
Like in Denmark

*Christen Anders Christensen was a teenager when he, his father, and his
brother Christian left Denmark to embark on a trip to Minnesota, USA,
and then on to Wetaskiwin, Alberta, in the early 1900s.[1] In this memoir,
Christen reminisces about his travelling experiences by train and ship,
and highlights the various groups of people who were immigrating to
North America from Europe. He also recounts his family's lack of funds
and the need for him and his siblings to take on paid employment.*

◾

I was just sixteen. Father took us to Horsens, Denmark, and on the
road a black cat crossed our path, I remember. I made my first railway
trip, through very hilly country at first, and further westward through
flat windswept country to Esbjerg. Standing on the packet [ship] that
evening, I watched, through tears, my country disappearing through
the evening haze. Would I ever return?

The North Sea can be very rough. The ship was small and slow,
an ideal place for seasickness, and the quarters were crowded. I
soon found out that we were classified as immigrants. The people
all around us were talking in strange tongues. In reality, they were
Swedes. One night, one day, and another night, and we found ourselves in calm waters, entering the port of Grimsby in England. The

quay was such a busy place, unloading our ship and others. There were big boxes of eggs, bacon, and butter.

The next day, a Sunday, we spent in Grimsby, watching an endless stream of people walking or promenading the whole day long. That was England. Grimsby had a whole street of houses with corners facing the street. A new town, it seemed to be.

A train pulled up with doors for every two seats. We were loaded in, the doors slammed shut, and we were en route for Liverpool, England, to take passage to Saint John, Canada, via the CPR ship the *Lake Erie*. In Liverpool, we stayed a week, waiting, I suppose, for the *Lake Erie* to unload cattle to make room for the immigrants.

While in Liverpool, we had to pass through inspection—really just a look in the eyes. A large number were crowded onto a board floor over a basement. All of a sudden, it collapsed into the basement. What a sight! Young and old struggled to get on even keel. Then we were piled into a courtyard with a high cement wall with broken glass on top and, one by one, were inspected and let out. It was there I got acquainted with the smell of garlic for the first time, as we were crowded in with Middle Europeans.

We were quartered in a big building on Hardy Street. Our beds were a couple of storeys up. I had a great time riding the stair railing up and down. But sleeping was a bit uncomfortable. We were three in a bed, I in the middle.

The *Lake Erie* was anchored way out in the open water, but finally everyone was aboard. Conditions on board were very crowded. The drinking water was horrible, and the food not much better.

The front end of the boat was full of Englishmen going to Canada to work on the railroad. The back end was packed with Russians—what are now called Ukrainians. They had a Danish cook, and I used to go to him to get some hardtack to supplement our fare. In the middle of the ship were some regular cabins where the Scandinavians were quartered. About twelve of us single Danes had only the floor for a bed. I made the mistake of taking my shoes off, and my feet suffered. Also on the boat was a row of cabins with doors, and portholes out to the open for first-class passengers. There was a group of black-robed nuns travelling in these. Were they ever lucky! I thought that if I ever went back to Denmark, it should be first class.

△ A family of Ukrainian immigrants in 1906. *Image NA-1000-9 by A.R. Wright. Courtesy of Glenbow Archives, Archives and Special Collections, University of Calgary.*

Crossing the Atlantic, we had constant headwinds, and it took twelve days. Fortunately, I was sick only one day in mid-ocean. Everybody was under deck, but we were often told to go up on deck.

On arriving at Saint John, we were led through endless railway yards to a restaurant. Then, we were packed into trains bound for Montreal, Quebec. This was about the only contact I ever had with New Brunswick and Quebec, but there was nothing much to see but a lot of blackened tree stumps.

In Montreal, Christian and I again came in contact with the Ukrainian immigrants. We were headed for Wisconsin, so were put aboard the Soo Line. We probably stayed on the Canadian side, because I remember the enormous railway yards at Sault Ste. Marie. We were nearing the end of the journey, a good thing. The food tasted very salty. The Danes were singing songs. One fellow, looking out the window, remarked, "Everybody looks so wealthy, wearing leather shoes."

We were left at Turtle Lake, Wisconsin, miles away from Milltown, our destination. Surprising, though, all our baggage was there.

We went to have dinner. Everything imaginable was on the table—all for twenty-five cents. A dinner fit for a king. A Swedish fellow told us how to board a train for Santa Cruz Falls. From there, we went by livery team to Milltown, a Danish settlement with a few Norwegian and Irish settlers too.

My brother Thomas was not there to meet us. He had previously gone to Canada looking for a homestead. I got a job working for Mads Bank in a feed and planing mill, and was lucky at that. Christian went out on a farm at twenty dollars per month and did two men's work, such as milking twenty cows in about two hours.

At the mill, we had a horse, Flora, and a cow. Mads Bank was very happy that I could milk the cow and feed the horse. A young Swede taught me every swear word in about a week. Their meaning I never knew, nor did I ever used to swear in Danish.

I learned many things, such as tying sacks with speed, looking after the planer, and carrying lumber till my shoulders got pressed down. In winter, it was very cold and the snow was three or four feet deep. It was a cold job for my fingers, tying sacks, and I kept my ears warm with a woollen toque.

Life here was not like in Denmark. In the spring, the roads would actually spring like rubber under the wagons. In summer, the days were hot and the nights even hotter. After sunset, it quickly got dark, not like in Denmark, where you could see clearly through the night for forty days.

Early in the summer of 1903, the rest of the family arrived from Denmark, including Mother and two sisters, Helen and Anna. Thomas had been in Alberta, looking over the homestead situation. He finally arrived back in Milltown after a very unusual journey. Being short of money, he had to beat his way. When the conductor on the train came to collect the tickets, Thomas would go off to the washroom or the space between the cars. Then he would catch the conductor alone and bargain with him for a tag to a certain point for so many dollars, strictly an underhand deal. He made it for a while with various conductors, but finally one of them lost his temper and kicked him off the train, none too gently. He must have tried again, for he arrived.

Then, Father and Thomas had to decide whether to stay in Wisconsin or go to Alberta. Thomas already had a homestead of

160 acres in sunny Alberta, a wonderland where people never got sick. He urged the family to go with him to Alberta and take out a homestead. The folks had got settled on a farm [in Milltown] and had a team, some cows, and furniture. It was a cruel decision to make. But Father was used to a big acreage. Where the family lived, there was only forty acres partly broken; the rest was in big stumps and pasture. Finally, Father decided to go.

There was some talk of $1,100 that was left over when everything was squared away in Denmark, but it seems to me that before starting for Alberta, Father had just $300. Whatever it was, he had to watch his spending. The stock and household effects, and also some lumber, was loaded into a freight car, and Thomas was to travel with them free. And so the heroic adventure began. Helen, Anna, and I were to stay in Wisconsin to earn a little money. I was still getting fifteen dollars a month. Helen was placed with the Ducholms at Bone Lake, a big farm and a big family. Anna was actually left behind in order to be confirmed by the Danish minister and was placed for wages with Jens Hermensen, who was running a store and butcher shop, and also served meals. The work, such as turning the meat grinder, was too heavy for a child, and she got rheumatism in her arms. She suffered a lot and had to take electric treatments. Finally, Mads Bank came to her rescue and moved her down to his place.

In the summer of 1904, Anna and I came to Alberta. Anna was fifteen and I was seventeen. Helen stayed in Minneapolis to work. Anna and I travelled on an immigration train. Travelling through St. Paul and Minneapolis on the Soo Line, we went through the most beautiful parts, something that did not happen to us again for a long time. We entered Canada at [an entry] portal. From there, we travelled CPR through what is now Saskatchewan. I don't remember noticing anything in particular but prairie, and funny little gophers. Hardly any of the land was cultivated. Some deep furrows running north and south at regular intervals turned out to be buffalo trails, I was informed. There were lots of white buffalo skulls almost everywhere at that time.

How we passed the long journey, I don't understand. We had no company, not knowing much English, but I don't remember the trip as being tiresome. Eventually we reached a small town. Mr. Swanson, the immigration agent who sort of looked after us, told us this was Calgary, a name very new and funny to us. I did not try to pronounce it. The same can be said of Red Deer, which was quite a busy place it seemed, since in every door a bell was ringing vigorously, inviting passengers to dinner.

Father was in Wetaskiwin to meet us, be he praised. But my gun and baggage had not arrived. We soon saw that Wetaskiwin had a lot of Swedes and a lot of saloons. We stopped overnight at Wodeen's boarding house.

When I arrived at the homestead, I was really not impressed with my future home. Although the house was framed, it had studs of poplar inside for walls. But it was home, with familiar things inside it that Father had hauled in many loads from the railway at Wetaskiwin, and the family was all there, except Helen. Mother and Father always kept open house and there was lots of company, with good things to eat. And so my life in this country began.

▼ A prairie gopher in 1914. *Image* NA-5262-109. *Courtesy of Glenbow Archives, Archives and Special Collections, University of Calgary.*

Sandra Rollings-Magnusson

Building a Bloc Settlement

Leopold Lippert, his wife, and children were Moravians (a group of German Protestants) from Russia who immigrated to Canada in 1894 to become homesteaders.[1] They were a very poor family who suffered through illness, economic and physical hardship, and near-starvation, before their life on the western prairies began to improve. Even though they came as part of a bloc settlement and had others to rely on from time to time, their strong religious convictions were what helped them to persevere.

■

After enduring some of the hardest days and years of my life under the heavy yoke of Russian oppression, both spiritual and physical, I finally broke away on May 10, 1894, from Volynia in Russia and set out for Canada, together with other brethren and sisters. Altogether, we were fourteen families.

The brother who originally planned this exodus, Andreas Lilge, had gone on ahead a year earlier and had succeeded in negotiating reduced transportation rates for us with the Canadian government. For the poorest of our number, he had even secured free passage.

In view of the fact that, in our group, I was considered most conversant with the Russian language, the responsibility of securing all the passports for the entire company devolved upon me. I also had much to endure on the voyage over because I had to take care of the

whole group. At the same time, I had to look after my wife, who was nearly blind and was expecting childbirth, and had to keep an eye on our six children, the oldest of which was only twelve. In my pocket, I had twenty rubles of Russian money.

After a journey of five days by wagon and rail, we reached the seaport town of Libau [Latvia], on the Baltic. Here, we had to lie over for thirteen days, waiting for our ship to sail for Hull, England. By that time, most of my twenty rubles were eaten up. Altogether, fifteen days were spent on shipboard. The difficulties I had to endure on the water cannot be described. My wife, as already stated, near childbirth; a four-year-old boy running a constant temperature; myself on my feet day and night until I broke down and was practically unconscious for five days. But in all my suffering, I trusted in the Saviour.

After twenty-seven days of travel, we finally arrived in Winnipeg. I had one dollar left. For three days, we stopped in Winnipeg, and then we continued our way to Edmonton. When we were about to

Sandra Rollings-Magnusson

leave Winnipeg, I had thirty cents in my pocket. I went downtown and bought thirty cents worth of bread. A certain woman gave me a can of syrup, worth twenty-five cents. On this food we subsisted till we got to Edmonton—I with three of the children. My wife, practically blind, was kept in the Winnipeg Hospital for treatment. After a week's time, she was sent on to Edmonton, not a bit improved.

After our arrival in Edmonton, our first thought was, on what will we live here? We had no money. We had nothing! But the good Mennonites in Manitoba had provided. They had shipped a half-carload of food and other necessities on to Edmonton in advance of our coming, and when we arrived, we found flour, some meat and bacon, and even old clothing.

On the second day, we set to work. The flour had to be unloaded from the boxcar, but because our original company had been broken up on the way, there were only four men at Edmonton for the time being, and we were in an exhausted condition. It was hard work for famished men to move such heavy sacks of flour. Moreover, our leader, Andreas Lilge, began to manifest for the first time his barbarity. He revealed himself as a veritable slave-driver. All day long we carried the flour, with scarcely a break. By 6 PM we were finished.

Meanwhile, the sisters prepared some flour soup, and we refreshed ourselves a little. Then we wanted to lie down and rest a while. But our inconsiderate leader broke in upon our rest and gave us orders, "You must start for your homesteads at once." He said that he had reserved a Township of land for us with the Canadian Immigration Department, and he wanted us to go at once and inspect it. We told him that we were too tired, and besides that, we wanted to wait till the rest of our party arrived from Winnipeg. "No," he replied. "You must start tonight. I have hired a rig for tomorrow and will follow you." So we had to leave that very night and go out into the strange world, scarcely knowing whither.

In a general way, he told us in which direction to walk. We objected that we had no food to take along and would starve on the way. Then one of the sisters came up and said that they had just baked a quantity of bread and each of us could take two loaves—that is, three of us, for the fourth man remained at the immigration shed in south Edmonton, where we were quartered.

After we were gone some distance, we came to a fork in the road and asked ourselves, "Which way shall we take?" We decided to turn to the right. At length, we came to a shack. We awakened the occupant to ask him for directions. He was an Englishman and we could not talk a word of English. But we knew that we had to get to Fort Saskatchewan. So we spoke that name, and he then gave us to understand that we were on the wrong trail. He went outside with us and pointed straight north across the open country, and by sign language indicated that, after a time, we would have to turn to the right. We followed his directions as best we could and ultimately came in sight of the fort.

We had now gone eighteen miles, but at this point we had to cross the Saskatchewan River in order to actually get to the post. The fare at that time was twenty-five cents, and I didn't have a cent. The other brethren had enough for themselves but could not help me out. What now? Would I have to remain behind and return to Edmonton? While we were considering our plight, a German farmer came along with a load of hay. He suggested that I should crawl up on his load and hide in the hay so that the ferry-man could not discover me. The driver assured me that as long as he had to pay ferriage for his hay anyway, I might as well steal a ride. So I followed his suggestion, but afterwards had severe compunctions because of the fraud.

From Fort Saskatchewan, we had to walk another sixteen miles. One of the other brethren had a shotgun, and as we scarcely could swallow our dry bread any longer, he shot a couple of the little rabbits that we saw on the prairie. We built a fire and roasted them at the flame. I could not eat any of the meat. In fact, I had not eaten anything since we left Edmonton.

Across from the place where we camped, there was a house in which, as it turned out, a German family by the name of Krebs was living. The man came over to investigate who the wayfarers might be. When he learned that we were Germans, he seemed to be glad. Finally, he asked me whether I was sick, for he noticed that I was not eating like the rest. I answered, "No, not yet, but I was beginning to feel that way. I cannot eat this heavy food." He then went back to his house and brought out a large dish of milk. That was like a healing balm to my sick stomach. I shall never forget the man's kindness, done to me in my great need.

The following morning we arrived at our destination. Our leader was there likewise and also the land inspector. After crossing the Township in every direction, we did not find enough suitable homesteads to go around. So we had to select some on an adjoining Township. Thereby, we became widely separated, so that we were from one to five or more miles distant from each other.

While tramping about on this land hunt, I became very sick. As mentioned before, I could not partake of any food. Such provisions as we had were not suitable for my weak stomach. Moreover, our bread was all consumed and there was nothing left for our party to do but to shoot rabbits and hawks and to fry them at the fire. At night, we had to lie down on the bare ground, without covering of any kind. In the morning, the grass was white and stiff with hoarfrost, though this was July. After we had canvassed the Township, I had to be taken back as a sick man to Edmonton in the hired rig, while our leader sat in with the inspector.

After arriving in Edmonton and having some cooked food—even though it was nothing more substantial than thin flour soup—I began to feel better. Two weeks had now elapsed since our arrival at the immigration shed, and the authorities in charge informed us that we would have to vacate our quarters, for other settlers were arriving and needed our accommodations. Besides, all our flour was still stored in the building and increased the crowded conditions of the hall.

A new difficulty now arose. It became necessary to divide the flour among the various families. Each family was to receive ten sacks, but because I had to borrow the ten dollars necessary to file on my homestead, I had to sell four of my bags, leaving me only six. I also received a ham. Our leader kept the largest portion to himself—fifty sacks of flour, besides a lot of bacon, beans, peas, grits, etc. The rest of us did not get any of these things.

But the greatest problem was how to get our supplies out to our homesteads. We had no team and no money to hire one. But, again, our merciful Saviour helped wonderfully. One of the older brethren, who still had a little money left from the Old Country, bought a yoke of oxen and an old wagon and then transported as much as he could.

He also took my stuff, as well as my wife and children, and away we went! Others borrowed some horses from a rancher, and so we finally got all our goods to our respective places.

How we fared after we got there is hard to describe. As already mentioned, our farms lay far apart. Everyone had to get his family and his belongings to his own place as best as he could. Everything had to be carried. Brother Heffner and I built ourselves a little hut together, constructed of stout poles, laid some grass on the rafters, and moved in. To enter, you almost had to crawl on all fours. My wife's eyes grew worse. She cried day and night. She lost one eye entirely. A two-year-old boy got the measles and also became blind in one eye. There was no doctor to be had, no help of any kind. In the midst of all this, my wife gave birth to a son. A few days later, Mrs. Heffner also had a baby—both in the same rude way and with all the children around. It was heartbreaking. And nothing more to eat than a little flour. Brother Heffner had bought a stove, and that was a big help. Fortunately, it was a rainless summer. Otherwise we would have perished under the open skies.

We now had to go into the woods and hew logs for our winter house. Everything had to be brought together on our backs and shoulders. In the midst of our operations, our leader came along and told us that we would have to build his house first. Meanwhile, winter approached and our flour began to give out. Then the good Lord sent us rabbits. In the evening when we went outdoors, we could see hundreds of them—yes, big droves of them. So we dug some deep pits, put some twigs across the opening, strewed a little hay over the top, and when the rabbits came out at night to feed on the hay, they dropped through the covering and fell to the bottom of the pit. In the morning, everyone went to his pit and got the "manna" out—seven or eight rabbits in one haul. Once, someone asked a brother, "Well, how many did you get last night?" "Oh," was the reply, "only fifteen." Such were the wonders of grace which the Lord performed. And yet, after a protracted, steady diet of rabbits, often eaten without seasoning or salt, we had to contend against the ingratitude.

When the flour was all used up and the rabbits were no longer fit for food, I went away to look for settlers who might like to have some work done. Twelve miles from home, I found a family of English

Trapping rabbits in 1910. *Image NA-2219-3 by C. Arneson. Courtesy of Glenbow Archives, Archives and Special Collections, University of Calgary.*

people. I showed them by signs that I was looking for work. I could not talk, but they understood my meaning. So they gave me something to do. They took me out into the field and showed me a place where they wanted me to dig a cellar. The ground was still frozen. I had to use the pickaxe to work with. After digging for some days, I began to feel so uneasy about my family that I must go home. The people gave me forty pounds of flour and a pig's head. With these provisions, I started off on my twelve-mile jaunt. The snow was two feet deep and there was no well-broken path. About two miles from my home, I was so exhausted that I could not go any further. I sat down in the snow and began to weep, alone in the wilderness. I tried to get on my feet, and, sure enough, my attempt was successful. I could move my feet forward. I took up my bundle, which had become thrice as heavy as at first, and eventually was able to reach my home.

As soon as my children spied me, they all rushed out to meet me and rejoiced greatly over the flour and the pig's head. They had had nothing to eat for the last twenty-four hours, and if one of the sisters had not brought them a little rye flour, I might scarcely have found them alive. My little Carl had said to his mother, "Why don't you go to the well and pull some food up, like you draw water?"

After we were here for a year, the good Mennonites loaned each of our families two cows and two oxen. Then our troubles were alleviated. We were grateful for the help, and after five years we paid for the stock. They also sent us another carload of flour and provisions, some seed grain, and a number of old ploughs and harrows.

I have written the most essential facts in this account. To give all the details would lead too far. The Saviour be praised for his wonderful leading hitherto. May He help us all to continue to build His Kingdom and to live for Him, for He has gathered a people for Himself among the despised Russians, upon whom many looked down and did not consider them capable of becoming, by God's grace, what they have become.

True Grit

*In this memoir, Cecilia Hryzak Kissel tells of the difficulties faced by
her Ukrainian family and friends, who wished to homestead near
Edmonton, Alberta.[1] Problems arose when they learned that officials from the Dominion Lands Office wished them to settle as a
bloc settlement in the Fish Creek area of Saskatchewan. Cecilia sets
out the conflict that occurred and how it was finally resolved.*

All my life, I have known and understood that there are two sides to
every story. After those who were minor nobility had emigrated to
Canada came others who did not have the finances, proper direction,
or instructions as to when to emigrate. Some barely scraped together
the price of the fare, 150 florins or rinksi (sixty dollars) per adult. They
came in the fall to a bare homestead. Their little dugouts with poles
leaning from the ground, being A-shaped, then branch covered and
mudded over, were not satisfactory for more than a few days of summer camping. It was unsatisfactory for severe, fifty degrees below
zero weather.

People coming with empty hands, empty pockets, no garden produce, a limited amount of clothes or household necessities gave cause
for much concern to the Canadian authorities.

I have some stories of the birth of Minnedosa–Riding Mountain
Colonies in Manitoba. These colonies were formed around May of

1899, were soon peopled by tenacious immigrants, grim and firm with purpose to succeed in this, bettering their future and that of their descendants.

I remember numerous accounts as described by my grandfather and his cousins, which did happen in those early days. Peasants who could scrape together only passage money arrived with their families, but with very little of this world's goods. It appeared that at the Winnipeg Immigration Hall, no one clapped their hands, and, in fact, they took umbrage.

What added to this problem was the inappropriate time of their arrival—late fall. In 1898, during the colonization of Fish Creek, difficulties presented themselves. Some people are never delighted when another tells them where to go. From our family lore and actual documentation, we have confirmation that C.W. Speers (a western immigration agent) hoped to settle some families in Fish Creek. It was their intention to go to Edmonton, Alberta, and Silton, Saskatchewan. They wanted what they wanted. Mr. Speers wanted what he wanted.

Mr. Speers did not inform the immigrants of the proposed destination. They arrived in Saskatoon, then learned that they were going to Fish Creek. Now disenchanted, they bucked and wanted to go to Edmonton, where their relatives were, refusing any discussion of other destinations. Seeing some of them begin to walk back to Regina gave Speers cause for concern. Speers wired to Winnipeg for advice in this dilemma. He concluded that he was baffled and defeated. It just proves that these Ukrainians had true grit.

Speers wired to McCreary in Winnipeg.[2] The North West Mounted Police Commissioner, Lawrence Herchmer, wired McCreary in Winnipeg, placing his call from Regina. The message was the same, "These Galicians refuse to locate in Fish Creek."

McCreary also appealed to the Commissioner of the North West Mounted Police, who dispatched a sergeant and two men, who would assist in the Fish Creek colonization dilemmas as they occurred. Of course, McCreary made the trouble in the first place. He should have known that, when these settlers learned they were deceived and could not join their relatives, they would make themselves understood.

These directors or commissioners could only see their side of the issue and complained about the turbulent Galicians! At least thirty families went to Edmonton, and seventeen families went to Silton.

On May 21, 1898, Commissioner McCreary, accompanied by Cyril Genik and Philip Harvey, arrived in Saskatoon and proceeded to Rosthern (a town located in the vicinity of Fish Creek), now five years old [to check on the colonization of the area]. McCreary, of course, still wanted the immigrants to go where he told them to go. He now evolved a gem of a plan. "You cannot imagine the difficulties there are, to get these people to go to a new place. It has to be done either by force or deception," he grumbled to Frank Pedley [the Superintendent of Immigration in the federal government] at Ottawa.[3] "They cannot be allowed to select for themselves where they are going. There must be some means of compelling them to go where the government agents select."

Finally, it was decided to meet the settlers at Halifax with Cyril Genik and learn where the settlers already had close relatives. As for others, perhaps they could be persuaded to see reason and agree to go to Fish Creek.

This writer feels close affinity for those with whom McCreary had so many problems, and also those who did stay and colonize at Fish Creek. It was my Hryzak forebears who came, just a month later, to settle in Fish Creek.

Lost Luggage

In this memoir, Annie Condon recalls leaving her beloved Ontario home behind to follow her husband to the western prairies.[1] She describes in detail the four days that she and her six children spent on the CPR and Canadian National Railway (CNR). Not only does she remember the difficulties they encountered, but she also comments on the beauty of the passing scenery as well as the kindness of strangers who helped her during her travels. Joy was experienced once she finally met her husband and son at the railway station in Invermay, Saskatchewan, at the end of their journey.

Thomas W. Condon was a blacksmith and was settled comfortably at Kingsmill, Ontario. The house he owned was an old-fashioned frame house with a climbing rose over one front window and a dark red bush rose beneath the other. A terraced lawn with a border of flowers each side of the walk; two small evergreens stood a short distance from the gate; inside the fence and between the lawn and line fence was a large clump of Golden Glow that bloomed abundantly, nodding their blossoms in the breeze. There were also beds of flowers, among them a beautiful bed of pansies which I prized highly. The following poem will explain what happened to them. My four-year-old wanted to give them to me:

She looked so sweet with her apron full
From my beautiful pansy bed.
I was so shocked when I saw them there,
Then I looked at my darling's face so fair,
And I only smiled instead.
"See, Mama! Pitty flowers," she said,
As we gazed on their beauty rare.
"Yes, Darling, I see," I quickly replied
As I tried to forget how it looked outside,
In my barren pansy bed.
Her face was so full of happiness
O'er the treasure she had brought,
I could not mar the joy in her eyes,
So I feigned that I was quite surprised,
And pretty bouquets we wrought.

The blacksmith's shop was at the corner of our three-quarter-acre lot, rows of small fruit of various kinds, in line with fruit trees just coming into bearing, between which was an excellent garden, several rows of strawberries, and a row of beehives.

The schoolhouse was just across the road, where we had a good attendance at Sunday school and an afternoon service, also. There were excellent neighbours that I dearly loved, a home where I was happy and content. In 1905, the excursions to the new provinces of Saskatchewan and Alberta attracted so many,[2] and before I realized it, my husband had caught what was commonly termed "the North-West fever," and closing his shop, he left on a harvest excursion for Weyburn, Saskatchewan.

He was delighted with the country and the wonderful crops, especially the wheat—acres and acres of golden grain so tall and vigorous. The morning of his arrival, he was offered a situation as a blacksmith at twenty-two dollars per week, which was good wages at that time. This he accepted, and stayed two months. A former acquaintance took him for a drive around his six hundred acres of the finest wheat he had ever seen. The glowing accounts convinced me I would have to go and, rather unwillingly, I consented.

In March 1906, we made a sale and oh, how it hurt to give up my cozy home and furniture! It had to be done. My husband said, "I will never be satisfied until I get a farm. I have always wanted one, and now is my chance." After the sale, I was moved to Clear Creek, my childhood home, to be near my people. A house was rented not far distant, and some new chairs bought, which mother took in return for milk and eggs. We reserved a heater and the much-needed sewing machine. Living near mother was like a long visit, and many of my girlhood friends visited me there. Near the end of March, Mr. Condon went, taking our eldest son Willie with him, who was now fourteen. He could help considerably in erecting buildings after they found a location that suited.

He bought tickets for Edmonton as he was advised to go up the new line of the CNR. But he got off at Canora, Saskatchewan, and decided not to go much further. The homesteads were taken around Canora, so he went to Invermay. Land seekers came in such numbers, they were obliged to sleep on the boarding house floors and in the hayloft of the livery barn.

He looked about and finally left Willie there and went to Quill Lake, where he had a good offer if he would blacksmith in that town, but he did not like the looks of white crusts of alkali on the soil, and he went on to Vonda. But that did not look as good as Invermay, so he went back there and bought a lot for one hundred dollars and began to build.[3]

The first blacksmithing he did was with borrowed tools under a slender poplar tree on the Archie Campbell farm. His tools, sent long before, had gone astray, and no trace of them could be found until June, when he got a refund on their tickets and located the tools at Humboldt. He was ready for work in July in his neat frame shop. The country was too new for much work, and oxen were used instead of horses that we were accustomed to in Ontario.

The townsite was covered with a dense growth of tall, slender poplars, with pussy willows in low places. Both house and shop were almost finished, so he got the job of clearing the streets. Bonfires at night delighted the children and young folks, and finally, all streets were cleared, though the stumps were still there. The streets were laid out and named while they were still covered with trees, which no doubt had to be done that way by the surveyors, but it did seem strange to me.

We were on First Avenue. Another lot was bought and a man hired to break the land for the first garden in Invermay. It was not a wonderful success, but produced some good vegetables. The soil was rich, black loam, but so full of roots and shaded too much by tall trees on each side. Not thinking of frost when a cool night came, we lost a fine crop of green beans. With the crop of potatoes, turnips, and onions, planted before I came, on an old camping ground across the creek, we would have a good supply, as the crop looked promising I thought when I arrived, which was on the eighth of June.

I left Clear Creek on the fourth. My brother, Freeman, took us to Port Burwell, driving a team and a two-seated open carriage we called a democrat. A wagon brought the trunks and household goods I wanted to take. How often I wished I could have gone with Mr. Condon and Willie! It was such a long trip to take with six children, and baby was only six weeks old the day I started via CPR from Port Burwell to Toronto, where I was to get a tourist car or sleeper for the remainder of the trip to Winnipeg, where I had to change and travel by CNR to Invermay.

Having so many little folks who needed sleepers and changes of clothing, I packed a bagful and put it under my seat where I could get it if needed. The conductor said it must go out in the baggage car, so I gave it up without asking for a check. He said I could easily get it in Toronto, but I did not find it easily as it was hard to leave the little folks and I had no check. A Traveller's Aid kindly offered assistance, and Charlie accompanied her, but that great Union Station was so filled, it was like hunting for a needle in a haystack, and our train had to pull out without it. I had only a small basket with a few articles for my baby and not one extra dress. Our large lunch box had also been taken out at the conductor's request, but I sent Charlie after it, as I knew we would need our lunch before reaching Toronto. On opening it, the first thing I saw was the fifty dollars I had placed there in a hurry. I was not long in getting it into my stocking, where I initially intended to put it.

There were eleven children in that tourist car, and I put baby's cloak on for a dress while I washed and dried his dress in the small kitchen. We also had a table hooked on the wall that helped me serve lunch from my box, which I might have lost with the money as well as lunch. A fierce thunderstorm and worry about my lost baggage kept me from sleep. Next day I sent a description of the lost baggage from North Bay, Ontario, and asked to have it forwarded to Invermay. It was several days coming and $4.50 in charges, but I was so glad to get it! It would be hard to replace as there would be so much sewing to do—even my good dress and the girls', besides all baby's clothing and the little boys' summer suits and sleeping apparel. Although there were beds on the train, we were obliged to sleep in our clothes.

There were so many friends in a short time in the tourist car. Especially do I feel grateful to Mr. and Mrs. Cathcart of Chatham, whose destination was Regina. Either one would hold baby while I attended one of the other little ones or washed garments in the small sink. Mr. Cathcart gallantly served a cup of tea to me every time they had it. He got his teapot filled at the stopping places. This was an essential, they thought, for a nursing mother. The porter kindly left our berth until last, as I had to keep the girls in bed until their light waists or guimpes were dry, as they both wore jumpers.[4]

In spite of my troubles, I enjoyed the trip. Our fellow travellers were so kind, and my family were not much trouble. I received compliments on their good behaviour. One lady had her little one tethered to the seat. He would race up and down, and there was danger of his falling. My children were treated to oranges, candy, and even maple sugar, with the remark, "It would be a long time before they would see any more."

The scenery was fascinating. The rugged wilderness of New Ontario, pretty little lakes and streams, and rocks of different colours. Rowan bushes with bunches of red berries,[5] and several varieties of evergreen trees. Small towns and an occasional city. I thought Port Arthur was beautiful, and just across the river was another very pretty city, Fort William. Here was a great pier with large and small boats on each side. Large grain elevators on the shore, and logs by the thousand floating down the river. The hard clay and gravel roads made me think of my home at Kingsmill, Ontario.

From here everything took on a new interest as it was unfamiliar. As we were rounding a curve, we observed a great cloud of dust, and soon the train stopped. We then learned that a car was off the track—the dining car attached to ours. If it had been our car, some of the children would have been injured as it was impossible to keep them from running about. The dining car floor was literally covered with dishes, sugar, and various kinds of food. The crowd that was soon outside of the cars astonished me at the number one train can carry. The train was then divided, taking the first part and leaving us behind. A freight engine came to our assistance, and with great poles and plenty of muscle, the car was lifted back and we were off again after about a two-hour delay.

When our engine had returned, a heavy rain came on. The towering rocks and tunnels were not so frequent. As we neared Winnipeg, we could not go to bed, so we were sorry to have night come and shut off our view. Our new friends had gone to their berths after bidding us goodbye. Only a few of us who were to change trains at Winnipeg were up watching for the lights of the great city, "The Gateway to the North."

Though the little ones went to sleep, they did not cry when awakened. The porter carried Tommy to the bus, and the last we saw of our kind friends the Cathcarts was their waving hands as we drove away. They were to stop in Winnipeg for two weeks. Mr. Cathcart sent a telegram to inform my husband of our safe arrival in Winnipeg. We went to the Brunswick Hotel, where we were shown a room containing three beds, and soon we were sleeping soundly. It was still raining when we awoke next morning, and no comb or brush to be found, so we were obliged to go down to breakfast like a lot of tramps. After breakfast, Charlie went to a store and bought a comb, but we still had to appear in our soiled clothing. However, it could not be avoided.

Now came the hardest part of the trip. We had to wait until nearly two in the afternoon, as the CNR train did not leave until that time. The children were so restless and anxious to see their daddy and Willie! The train was so crowded that more coaches had to be added. At last, the train moved out, and I did not wonder at people speaking of the North-West being a wonderful country when I saw the rich black soil and wonderful crops all along the line. Tiny shacks were often seen now, with an occasional large house on a well-cultivated farm, and new towns not far apart with grain elevators, showing how productive the country was under cultivation. There were acres and acres covered with small poplar trees and pussy willows, also sloughs where wild ducks flew up by dozens at the sound of the train.

I will always remember the musical sound of the train whistle. The fourth night came on and we had no bed, as we expected Invermay before midnight, but train time had changed the day previous and we travelled all night, lounging in our seats. Our fellow travellers were very kind, treating the children, and an engineer from the Great Northern, who was holidaying with his brother, made a comfortable bed of his seat for little Susie, while they sat in the smoking car. He kept Bertha laughing, telling amusing stories about his little girl.

The prettiest town after leaving Winnipeg was Portage la Prairie, with its lovely maple trees and fields of raspberry bushes, not far from such beautiful residences. I was so glad to see this, after so much wild, uncultivated land. The next large place was Dauphin, where a great number got off. Morning broke about 3 AM. Watches were put back two hours from the eastern time. Trees became larger and more dense, and at 6 AM, we reached our destination, where Tom and Willie had watched nearly all night for the arrival of the train. How glad we were to see our loved ones once more.

Travelling in a Cattle Car

Minnie Taphorn offers a new adventure regarding her family's travels from the United States to the western prairies in 1906.[1] Rather than travelling in colonist cars, where benches and berths were available, her father and brother rode in a cattle car with their livestock and household belongings. She noted their experiences and how they tried to make the train ride as comfortable as possible. Minnie also sets out her family's priorities once their homestead was reached.

My dad (Fred) and my brother Carl left the United States in September 1906. We got an immigrant car and loaded our belongings, consisting of six horses, about seven head of cattle, pigs, chickens, and geese, also household furniture. My dad and my brother went with the car. They had plenty of food put up for on the trip. And also had plenty of quilts, blankets, and pillows. So when evening came, they made their bed close by the door of the car. They had a lantern hung from the ceiling of the car for light. Two or three barrels were taken along on the road with water for the cattle to drink. These were also placed by the door for easy filling. When the trains stopped at the station, the barrels were again filled with water, so water was always supplied. When they got into Winnipeg, my brother took the passenger train and went on ahead. It took my dad a little over a week to arrive in St. Gregor, Saskatchewan. My brother was there when dad arrived, so they waited till the next morning to unload. This way it saved an extra trip. An immigrant car had to be unloaded in twenty-four hours.

So early the next morning, they put the wagons together. They took all the cattle, horses, pigs, chickens, and geese, and the stove, food, water, barrels, and some furniture on the first two loads and started out for the homestead. The road was only a dim trail through the bush, a distance of seven miles south. There was no loading platform, so they made a kind of unloading platform for getting the cattle and horses unloaded. All there was in St. Gregor at that time was a section house. And Mr. Reise at that time had just started to build a store.

When they arrived at the homestead, the cattle and horses were first tied to the trees. Chickens and geese were left in the coops. They put the carpet over the wagon. This was their sleeping place till they got their building put up. The coyotes came close at nights and hung around the wagon. Guess they smelled the chickens.

They got the car unloaded in one day. When they had all things on the site for the buildings, they went to work and put the grass mower and hay rake together. They had to cut some hay for the cattle. There was plenty of grass to cut, so it did not take long. They could not turn the stock loose, or they would have wandered off and never been found. When some hay had been cut, my brother started off for Muenster, a distance of twelve miles at that time as the trail made a shortcut. Again, the only road was a faint trail, with more trails leading in different directions. All through heavy bush and prairie clearings.

Muenster consisted of a store run by H. Brunning and a Mr. Timbrook. The post office was also in the store. There was also a livery barn, hotel, and the lumber yard. The monastery started up in 1903. Carl bought his groceries and loaded his lumber and left for the homestead.

The old trail used to be south of the track up a steep hill. Sometimes it was hard for the horses to get a footing. In winter, when we went to Muenster, we left home at six in the morning with an open bobsleigh and a scoop shovel. Snow would be very deep in places, so if the horses got stuck in the snowbank, we used the shovel to make a path for them.

We needed a whole day going to Muenster, as days were short and the horses needed a rest before starting the trip for home. When my brother got home with the lumber, they started building a chicken barn first, as the chickens had to get out of the coops. Next came a shanty. It consisted of two rooms, twelve by sixteen feet, slant roof with tarpaper held in place by plaster lathes. The sides of the house were plain boards also covered with tarpaper. When it was finished, the furniture was moved in. There was a cookstove and big heater. Some more cupboards were made of boards so they could store things. This shanty was nice and warm in winter as there was plenty of wood to burn. Next came the building of the barn. It was also made of lumber, single ply. It was not very big, but the stock had shelter. Later on, a log barn was built against it.

Then they started making hay for feed for the winter. It was dry already, so they did not have to wait for the hay to dry. It could be raked right away. It was a nice fall, no rain or snow to bother them, so they got quite a bit of hay out, as it was a thick strand of grass. Then, when the hay was stacked, the digging of a well was started. They dug down fourteen feet and had plenty of good water. There was plenty of water in the sloughs, so they could water the stock before the well was done. Then they had to get wood for fuel out of the bush for the winter. It was close by. Later, in the winter, more wood was hauled to last all winter and summer.

Mother and I arrived in St. Gregor on November 18, 1906, at about five in the morning. There was no station and no station platform. Everyone had to jump from the steps of the train. This night was not the first snow, so the jumping was not so nice as we all landed in a deep snowdrift of loose snow.

The conductor was very nice. As my mother was kind of crippled, he carried her into the section house. The people living in the section house were friendly, too. They were poor and had nothing to offer us, but they did make us all a cup of black coffee. We waited till eleven o'clock in the morning, when my brother arrived with the team and sleigh to take us to our new home. Going home, we went through heavy bush and big trees. We arrived home good and hungry. My dad had a good hot dinner ready. It was sure good to get a hot meal again.

The Wedding Trip

*Edna Banks was a young woman from the bustling city of Toronto,
Ontario, keen on marrying her beau, Wilf, who had travelled to
Saskatchewan to homestead in 1910.[1] Recounting Wilf's experiences on the train, as well as her own when she decided to follow him,
Edna describes some of the difficulties each of them encountered with
this mode of transportation. She goes on to elaborate on some of the
unique incidents that she also faced along the way. Getting married
was memorable for her, as well as her first overnight stay at a stopping
place as she and Wilf travelled by horse and wagon to their homestead. Her first glimpse of her new home was also an unforgettable
experience, particularly her disappointment with its rustic flair.*

To those who had the pluck and courage to take a chance, the thought
of being able to acquire a homestead of 160 acres of land for the
very modest sum of ten dollars, with the opportunity of getting a
pre-emption,[2] an additional 160 acres for a similar amount of cash,
was attractive. That would make a nice farm of 320 acres of land just
waiting for the plough.

The homestead duties, required by the government before the
homesteader could prove up, were not unreasonable, but they were
necessary in order to shut out mere speculators and were only what
any new settler on a farm would expect to do if he were sincere in

wanting a farm to make a home. He was required to build a habitable building, and apparently size was unimportant because there were some very small houses or shacks. If the homesteader was satisfied to be able to get himself a stove, a table, and a bed in, the government was satisfied. He was required to break or plough ten acres of raw prairie each year for three years, and to live on his land six months of each year for three years.

Wilf Shaw daydreamed of such a farm. His farm! He saw his breaking plough turning over the brown, fertile soil, the furrow a mile long. He saw the large acreage of gold wheat rippling in the sunshine like the waves on the lake on a lazy, summer day; the harvest and threshing, with their bustling activity.

The idea became an obsession, and one morning at the breakfast table he startled his parents when he said, "I'm going to the West on the next harvest excursion train. I want to see the Prairie." There was excitement and hustle and bustle, cooking and washing and mending. A week later, his mother packed him a substantial lunch basket, and on a sweltering day in August, he left Toronto from the old Union Station on the longest passenger train that he had ever seen and was greatly amused at the two massive locomotives that were going to haul it.

The trains were crowded, and after passing through several cars, looking for a seat that he would not have to share with another person, he found the train so crowded that he decided he would have to share a double seat with two other young chaps.

"Those seats were just wooden slats and there wasn't a cushion on them. They were the hardest seats I ever sat on," he told me.

"What did you do about sleeping?"

"Sleep. That was hell. Just plain hell, and that is the reason why I left the train at Brandon."

"What about your meals? Did you get tired of cold lunches?"

"No. My mother's lunch was good, and if I had had a saucepan and some tea, I could have had tea with my meals down at the end of the car. There was a small square box-like stove in a cubbyhole of a kitchen where the passengers could boil water. Some made porridge and some even fried bacon. That made me hungry."

Wilf chuckled and said, "A nice little old lady gave me a cup of tea once when I was eating a sandwich. I told her it was a good cup of tea and that it hit the spot, and after that, she gave me a cup of tea whenever she had one."

When the train pulled into Brandon, some farmers boarded the train looking for harvest help, and Wilf, who did not like the idea of another night on the train, grabbed up his luggage and went looking for the job that was looking for him. He always thought that had been a lucky thing to do, and when he finished his job in Brandon, he started walking his way through Manitoba into Saskatchewan. Sometimes he worked for a few days, and sometimes he hitched a ride. All this helped him to make up his mind about settling in the West. He liked what he saw—the friendliness of the prairie people, and he saw that the prairie was rich in opportunities.

When he reached Moose Jaw, a bit weary but still dedicated, he went directly to the Dominion Lands Office and there ran into a first-class piece of luck. Two prospective homesteaders, like himself, were already making arrangements to go down to the south country to look over the land and, if they liked what they saw, pick out some pieces of land. They were glad to have Wilf with them. Some homesteaders filed blind, but Wilf hoped to choose his own farm.

The three men packed a supply of grub, mostly canned goods, a small tent, a horse blanket each, and some threshed oats for the horses into the back of a democrat, after taking out the back seat and leaving it behind, and on a bright and chilly morning, they headed almost straight south. By using a compass, they continued in that direction for three days and had no difficulty locating what they were looking for—the wooden stakes that marked the already surveyed railroad between Weyburn in Saskatchewan and Lethbridge in Alberta.

After they got themselves located in relation to the wooden stakes, and keeping as close to the surveyed railroad as possible, they travelled sometimes east, sometimes north and west, but never south, where there was an alkali slough that they wished to avoid, and began looking for the iron stakes that they would find on the northeast corner of each Section of land.

Even after locating the iron stakes, which was not easy at first, they often had trouble making out the Roman numerals that were engraved on each stake, which indicated the number of the Section.

∧ People were so eager to apply for entry to their homestead, there was a rush at the Dominion Lands Office first thing in the morning. Prince Albert, Saskatchewan, 1908. *Image A-4557-2. Courtesy of Provincial Archives of Saskatchewan.*

Wilf said that sometimes the stakes were so badly rusted that they could not be sure that they read them correctly.

At night, they slept on the ground in the small tent, each man wrapped in his own horse blanket. The horses were hobbled and turned loose, and in this way were able to graze and get food, but were unable to wander far.

They spent ten days driving back and forth, and had made notes on several pieces of land when they decided to return to Moose Jaw and the Land Titles Office as quickly as possible and register their claim. Until it was registered with the Land Titles Office, any person could file on it.

They found the Land Titles Office doing a land-office business and in a state of wild uproar and confusion. Homesteaders, impatient and disgruntled and wanting to file their claim, had to wait around for days awaiting their turn. Some sat on the Land Titles Office steps all night, hoping they would get into the office with the staff in the morning. Some even tried crawling through the window, and on some mornings, the crowd milling around the office door was so dense that the office staff could not get into their office until a way was cleared. Wilf Shaw was one who sat on the steps one cold night, and with others who were also reduced to strategy, took turns going to a restaurant for food and hot drinks. When each man returned, he again took his proper place in the lineup. Wilf registered his claim, not his first choice, but still a beautiful piece of land, then took the first train going to Ontario.

Wilf returned to Ontario and told me about the south Saskatchewan prairie, which he said was called the banana belt, and about the house he was going to build on his land the following spring. That winter, Wilf courted me and went to auction sales [to buy agricultural equipment and farm stock]. He never bypassed going to an auction sale if he had a leg to stand on, and I never knew what he was going to bring home. The winter passed quickly, and Wilf began making his plans and arrangements to go west once again.

On the morning that he was leaving, he had help loading the machinery and other settler's effects, which included a team of horses and a cow, into the boxcar that had been left on the railway siding by a freight train a couple of days before. When I heard the train whistle in the afternoon, I knew he was gone. It sounded very final.

He proved to be a good letter writer that summer, in spite of the difficulty he had getting his mail with any sort of regularity. He told me that the long freight train which left Toronto was made up entirely of boxcars of settlers' effects, all going to the three prairie provinces, that he didn't sleep well lying on bales of hay that he had in the car to feed the horses and cow, and that the cow got down and couldn't or wouldn't get up.

He and some men lifted the critter out of the car onto the ground, and one evening the train was standing on a siding but they had to lift her back in again. You never know when a cow is spoofing; they can be contrary, and nothing that Wilf did or said would persuade her to budge. When he arrived in Morse, there was still the long trek to the homestead. Fortunately, he heard of another homesteader who was going down to his claim at the same time, and both were glad to have company. The cow didn't make the trip to the homestead.

Because it was scarce, money was important to the early settlers on the south Saskatchewan prairie. Their venture was like a one-way street. Money, time, and effort were going one way, only into the development of the homestead, and it would be a year or two at least before the virgin prairie yielded any dividends on the investment, and it was for that reason—that money was not too plentiful with either of us—that I agreed to meet Wilf in the West and be married there.

I considered that we could spend our money to better advantage, and he seemed pleased. He told me that he would come back for me as soon as he was able if I wished it that way, or if I wanted a wedding. I did not! Weddings and funerals are a bore unless you are the bride or the corpse, and neither did I want the fuss and feathers or the expense of a wedding, and before he left in the spring of 1910 with his carload of settler effects, he suggested that I meet him in the West in the late fall of that year. He said that he would have a small house built and made comfortable for winter living.

When I expressed a wish to spend one more Christmas at home with my parents, he was willing, and we settled on a date in January when I would go west. That was a busy summer for me too, preparing things for my new home, sewing on a wedding outfit, doing some experimental baking and cooking. On Christmas Day, we were all keenly aware that it might be the last one that we would all spend together. There was a beautiful sadness, recalling little mannerisms and jokes that belonged just to our family and home. Family ties were welded more firmly together, and distance would bind us even closer.

The train on which I left Toronto's old Union Station was made up of day coaches only. I shared a double seat with an elderly lady, her married daughter, and her small child. I'm sure they must have wished that I had gone somewhere, and I would have if I could have, for there was no position in which any of us could sit or sleep but straight up.

I tried to get a sleeper the second night on the trip and was told there were no sleeping cars on that train, nor was there a dining car, at least until we got to Winnipeg. The third night was another bad night for sleeping, or else our nerves were becoming frayed. The train was noisy and rocked on its bed as it hurtled through the night, straining for more speed and screeching like a tortured spirit. The weary restlessly tossed and twisted themselves into all sorts of shapes and postures, trying too hard to be comfortable and get some sleep.

I opened our window and, with some difficulty too, closed it quicker than I had opened it, as there was a loud howl of protest as the frigid January night air blew in. The one gulp of fresh air that I swallowed was heady and gave me an idea. I looked at my watch. Four o'clock! Good! The timing was perfect. I picked up my valise that had not been disturbed or opened since it was carefully packed before I left home, and I lurched to the washroom, bumping heads or rumps as I swayed down the aisle with the roll of the train. That was the moment I'd been waiting for and planning for—why hadn't I thought of it sooner?—and I prayed that I would have the washroom to myself.

The Gods were with me, and before I left the train, about six o'clock in the morning, and still dark, I was dressed in all my wedding clothes, from an Alice blue velvet poke bonnet with blue ribbons that tied under the chin or under my left ear, right down to a pair of new kid, high-button boots that pinched my feet just a little, but made them look small and neat. I told myself that the boots would stretch, but they never did. My feet grew bigger, and the mark of Cain can still be felt and seen on my left big joint.

In between the bonnet and the boots, I pulled on a pair of long, over-the-knees, hand-knit, soft Andalusian wool yarn stockings, over a pair of Penman's ankle-length, pure wool combinations, and fastened all my 106 pounds into a pair of corsets with steel stays, which I modestly hid under one plain, tight-fitting, and one fancy over-all embroidery and lace-trimmed corset cover. At that time, nobody questioned the sanity or the waste of time of all the rigamarole. That's what ladies were and that was what ladies wore.

Today, I do question the sanity and courage of us all, and wonder how on earth I could have further burdened myself with at least two, maybe four, petticoats, when my thirty-six-inch-long, navy blue serge wedding skirt (and no mean weight) barely cleared the floor and dirty streets. Maybe my five-foot-and-one-quarter-inch frame did sag. A lace peek-a-boo blouse, that some parents considered bold and some considered downright indecent, and a long fur-lined coat completed my wedding outfit.

When I left the brightly lighted, overheated train, I stepped into a first-class Saskatchewan blizzard. The wind screamed, "Go Home!" and to tell the truth, I did have a brief, wild impulse to get back on the train, even if it was going in the wrong direction. The passengers who left the train when I did must have known where they were going. They disappeared very quickly, and the station platform was almost deserted when the conductor, who was just about to step back into the train, asked me, "Are you expecting some person to meet you?" When I saw a pair of long legs striding down the platform, I told him that I was. It couldn't be anyone else.

When Wilf caught up with me, he said, "So, you got here," and all I could say was "Hello." The moment was embarrassing. I was still swaying with the motion of the train, and I could not think of one suitable or sensible thing to say that was suitable for the occasion. "I'll look after your luggage later and we'll walk across the street to the Chinese restaurant and have breakfast now," Wilf said.

It was the first time I had ever been in a Chinese restaurant, and although I knew that our churches had sent missionaries over to China in an effort to swap cultures, I didn't exactly know what to expect. I soon learned that the Chinese in Saskatchewan were an honest, kindly, and respected part of any prairie community.

⌃ The interior of a Chinese restaurant in 1910. *Image ND-2-109 by B.S. Cameron. Courtesy of Glenbow Archives, Archives and Special Collections, University of Calgary.*

"I have made arrangements with the Reverend Dr. S. to marry us at high noon," Wilf told me. "And if this storm lets up, we'll head for the homestead in the morning, or would you rather stay around for a few days?" I was anxious to see my new home and told Wilf so, and when morning came, it was clear, bright, and bitterly cold, and we took the early morning train to Morse, where Wilf had left the horses and sleigh in the livery stable.

As my husband tucked me in the sleigh and wrapped another horse blanket around me, he said, "If the trail is good today, we should get to a stopping place along the trail before dark." He was right, and daylight was beginning to fade in the late afternoon (it fades early in Saskatchewan in the winter) when he pointed to a light, saying, "That

Sandra Rollings-Magnusson

will be the stopping place." All afternoon there had been no fences, no trees, no landmarks, and not many buildings, and we had not seen anybody on the trail. When we pulled into the yard, I could see a few sleighs sitting around. "Maybe some homesteaders going out," Wilf told me, or maybe going in, like we were.

A coal-oil lantern hung on a peg at the side of the door. Wilf helped me out of the sleigh and told me to go into the house. We both admitted that we were cold and hungry. "Just walk in?" That was a surprise. "Yes, go on in. I'll put the team in the stable and be right in."

In deference to the privacy of other people, I rapped on the door, then opened it and stepped into the warm air from a large cookstove. I could see and smell dinner cooking and realized that I was cold and hungry indeed. A pleasant-looking lady, her soft, brown hair falling in moist wisps over her forehead and around her ears, was working over the hot stove and smiled a welcome. She told me to hang my wraps on some pegs that were strung along the wall just inside the door. Some men were already eating at an oilcloth-covered table that stretched down the middle of the room, and when Wilf came in, we joined them at the table. Some nodded, but two bewhiskered, unkempt lads, who were eating with their heavy mackinaw coats on,[3] ignored us.

Wilf joined in the conversation when he commented on the very cold weather, Saskatchewan's number one topic, and the conversation continued to run in true western form. "Where are you from? Where are you going? Got a homestead away down there, have you?"

After everybody was catalogued, except the two boys who never spoke to anybody, Wilf inquired about the next day's trail. I knew that he was anxious about the trip to the homestead the next day because it was getting deep into no man's land, but I did not realize the situation well enough to be plagued by doubts.

It was not difficult to see that the house was just one big square box, with a thin partition dividing it into two rooms—one for cooking and eating and one for sleeping. After we finished eating, Rhoda's husband, Tom, went into the sleeping room and started teasing and fluffing up the featherbed ticks around the floor. Two ticks for each bed, one to lie on, one for covering.

This was really homesteading life, I thought, and then something hit me—everybody would be bunking on the floor together. Horrified,

▼ A group of men standing outside a stopping place in 1909. When travelling, people could stop and rest at these places for a few hours and get a bite to eat, or they could stay overnight. *Image NA-493-2 by W.D. Albright. Courtesy of Glenbow Archives, Archives and Special Collections, University of Calgary.*

frightened, and fighting mad, in about two steps I went to where Rhoda was washing dishes. "Where am I going to sleep?"

"You can sleep with me," she told me pleasantly.

"Oh, no, I must sleep with my husband." Bless her. Rhoda gave up her bed, the only real bed in the house. Where did Rhoda sleep? I do not know.

Before going to bed behind some thin gingham curtains in a corner off the dining area, I whispered into Rhoda's ear and asked about the toilet facilities, and she whispered back.

"Outside?" I gasped.

She nodded her head. "There is a path at the back of the house. It is down near the end of the yard."

"Judas Priest!" I snorted. Wilf nodded knowingly when I raised my eyebrows and glanced toward the door, and together we went out into the night and the cold and saw a brilliant display of the aurora borealis, blazing and flickering across the hard winter sky. The aurora borealis is especially magnificent in the West. The sunsets are unequalled for a gorgeous display of the delicate blending of many colours.

If I thought that my troubles were over for that night, I couldn't have been more mistaken, for the entire night was spent catching, and flinging out of the bed, those obnoxious pests that the Webster Dictionary defines as "small, wingless, biting insects," and beyond the thin gingham curtains were the most ludicrous conglomeration of noises one could ever hope to hear, snoring, gurgling, hacking, choking, belching—in every colour, tone, pitch, and volume.

There was no doubt in my mind I had not slept a wink all night, and when people began racketing around and I could hear pots and pans being banged around and men swearing at the weather, I knew

➤ TOP Homes were small and built out of whatever materials were readily available. In this photograph, a woman is sitting outside her tarpaper shack in 1900. Note the sod roof, the washboard leaning against the house, and the privy in the rear. *Image NA-4625-5. Courtesy of Glenbow Archives, Archives and Special Collections, University of Calgary.*

➤ BOTTOM A typical interior of a small one-room home on the prairies between 1910 and 1914. *Image NA-2487-2. Courtesy of Glenbow Archives, Archives and Special Collections, University of Calgary.*

it was supposed to be morning, although it was still black dark. If one could judge from the noises coming from the dining room and breakfast table, the overnight guests were eating with zest and still swearing about the weather. As each person finished his breakfast, he scraped his chair along the floor and banged out the door. We were the last to eat breakfast, and we too were on our way. All ships that pass in the night.

This was the last lap of our wedding trip, and as we pulled out of the yard and hit the trail, the sun, a brilliant red ball of fire, was just over the rim of the earth. There wasn't much conversation at that early hour, and I knew Wilf was thinking about getting us back home safely before dark, or we would be in serious trouble. We were travelling in the area where there were few people living since the ranchers moved out; the trail would be sketchy, and he was without benefit of fences or landmarks to guide him. All the world before and around us was snow-covered.

At noon, we stopped to eat a few sandwiches we had bought from Rhoda and to let the horses have a feed of oats and a rest, because the going was heavy in the untracked snow. Wilf cocked an eye toward the sun. "I think we are all right and it shouldn't be too far now."

After we were on our way again, it is the general opinion that I dropped off to sleep. When Wilf called, "Whoa! Whoa!" I wakened and he said, "Well, here it is."

I stared silently at the small house that was to be my home, sitting so alone, so unprotected in the middle of thousands of acres of snow, without even the protection of a coat of paint, and whose only address was a few Roman numerals on a weather-beaten iron stake. I opened the door. The inside looked lonely too. A cold cookstove stood just inside the door. I saw an unmade bed over in the corner, and a large kitchen table stood along the wall. The chairs were askew around the room. A packing box was nailed on the wall, which served as a cupboard for dishes, food, shaving articles, and just anything that needed a cupboard. Wilf reached into the cupboard and brought out one of the old-fashioned slow-lighting, slow-burning, hard-to-blowout matches that were in use at the time. We began piling frozen food and the water pail, which was a solid block of ice, on the top of the stove and in the oven and waited. Depressing, when you are cold and hungry.

Horse Thieves

*In this memoir, Charles Phillips sets out how he, his brother, and
their parents travelled by covered wagon from Montana, USA,
to the Canadian border at Coutts, Alberta, in 1910.[1] Their
travels were not without incident as they encountered snowdrifts on the trail, thieves who stole their horses in the night,
and a broken wagon wheel. Abandoning personal possessions
to lighten the load was also a difficult decision to make.*

◼

C.H. Phillips Sr. was office and station agent for the Great Northern
Railway when he learned of the vast land being opened for homesteading in Alberta, east of Calgary, in 1908. He became interested,
and in the late fall of that year he had the urge to investigate by taking
the train to Calgary, then on to the end of the steel at Stettler, which
would bring him within fifty or sixty miles of the open land for homesteading. The rest of the distance would have to be covered by foot,
as most newcomers had no other means.

After accomplishing the rugged adventure, for an office man, he
returned to his family, then living in Butte, Montana, with the good
news that he had filed on a homestead. How little did the family realize what a converted life this meant for them, but the venture was
accepted wholeheartedly by his wife and two sons: Glen, age seventeen, and Charles Jr., age eleven.

The next step was the planning for such an adventure and the method of transportation. It seemed quite logical that the best plan would be to purchase four horses and a covered wagon; thus, when we arrived at our location, we would have our covered wagon for shelter and the horses to accomplish the work that had to be done. Therefore, the balance of the winter was spent in securing horses that would be suitable and a mountain wagon that could be converted to a prairie schooner or covered wagon.

Dad was very handy at carpentry work, and after locating the desired wagon, he built a convenient and well-arranged covered wagon for our five-hundred-mile journey the following spring. This journey would take us through the Rocky Mountains and over the western plains with very few good roads to travel. The best you could call them would be poor trails, and just the survey stakes to guide you.

By the end of March 1909, the horses had been bought, the covered wagon was in readiness, the days in the valley where the city lay were bright and warm, and, apparently, the family was going to get off to a good start. The beginning of April and the equipment all loaded in the covered wagon, the family bid their friends and neighbours of the city farewell and started out of the valley and up the long grade to the Continental Divide. The grade was a long hard haul, but there was very little trouble encountered until we reached Elk Park, Montana, where we found the roads covered with snowbanks four feet deep. Consequently, these drifts had to be shovelled out before continuing. It was also found that our covered wagon was too heavily loaded for such road conditions, and we would have to continue with just bare necessities and abandon our keepsakes.

This was quite an ordeal for the family that had always had all the modern conveniences and comfort in their past life, and now calling it home wherever the covered wagon stopped for the night, whether stuck in a snowdrift, mudhole, or camping on a mountain ledge. Well, Dad's determination and energy seen us through the snow in about four or five days, though we had only travelled twenty-five miles on our way, but now we were over the Divide and down travelling in the valleys, where the beauty of spring was appearing. Apparently, we were going to make some progress, which we did for the next couple

of days, but in those days there was not the law and order to protect people from swindlers, especially in Montana.

After our couple days of successful travelling, and when evening came, we stopped where there was grass and picketed out our horses for the night. It was my chores then as a boy to gather the wood and carry the water, while Mother prepared the meals on a stove that was set up in the covered wagon. That night, we retired and felt relaxed and thought our worries were over—that is, for the time being anyway. By this time, we were accustomed to the bunk beds, and I don't think anyone awoke until the sun was shining through the canvas of the covered wagon the next morning.

Dad was always the first one to get up and start a fire and warm the canvas house up for the rest of us. To his surprise, all of our horses were gone when he looked out of the wagon. On making a further inspection, it was very obvious the horses had been stolen, or let loose by someone, as the picket ropes were still there, but the horses had been untied, thus leaving us afoot. But a thief can't always win.

Their game was that they knew that if the travellers were stranded long enough, the traveller would offer a reward for the return of his horses. We were fortunate. As luck would have it, one of the horses was shod with barred shoes, and as it was in the spring, the ground was soft and the horse left the print of his foot wherever he stepped. This made it easy for my dad and brother to trace where the horses had been taken, which was about five miles from camp, corralled in a small canyon.

By mid-afternoon, we had our horses back in harness and we were on our way again. The rest of the road to Helena, Montana, was rough and rugged, like all mountain roads were in those days, and we became very cautious of all the steep grades. The common practice for a mountain teamster was to rough lock his wagon going down and always be prepared for the worst going up grade. Dad soon became a first-class horse teamster with lots of nerve, which he had to have to take us over the roads and ford the rivers we were forced to cross.

After arriving in Helena, Montana, Dad was informed that our road ahead was too bad to continue for at least two weeks, so there was no alternative but to stable the horses and make camp and wait until the roads were passable. In the meantime, my dad and brother took on small odd jobs, which helped to finance the delay. After the two weeks' delay, the roads became passable and we could continue, but there were some restrictions and alterations decided on. The alteration was that just Dad, Mother, and I would continue with the horses and covered wagon. That decision was taken because my brother, Glen, had been offered a good paying job at the Yellowstone National Park for the summer, and by him taking that on, he could help promote the adventure on the road and when we arrived to the homestead in Alberta.

I know we all felt somewhat downhearted when we left the city of Helena to continue our way without Glen, but we also knew that it was our father's sole ambition to see his family comfortably settled on a farm, and an opportunity for his boys. Now, as to the restrictions, our first intentions were to travel from Helena to Great Falls, Montana, as that was the best-travelled road at that time, but Dad was advised to bypass Great Falls. Apparently, there had been trouble in those parts and that was what we desired to avoid and not invite.

Our first part of our travels would take us out through the Prickly Pear Canyon, that is, from Helena. We were only on the road for a part of a day when a wheel broke and disabled us until we could get a replacement. Fortunately, there was a sheep rancher not too far away that was kind enough to loan my dad a wheel that would take us to the next little village, which was called Wolf Creek, where we got our own wheel repaired and the rancher's wheel shipped back. While Dad was helping the blacksmith repair the wheel for our wagon, I was given the chore of watching the horses feed on a hillside and not let them get too far away. The canyon was well named, as I have never seen such huge and brutal cactus, or prickly pear, since. If you accidentally stepped on one of the needles, it would go through your shoe leather and pin your foot to the shoe.

It was while I was herding our horses in such a pasture, I noticed a .22 rifle lying on the ground, partly covered with grass and leaves. It had been there for some time. Dad worked on cleaning the rifle up in the evenings, and I soon had a gun of my own that I could shoot small game along the road, which helped out on the meat diet.

With the wheel repaired, and all things in travelling shape, we were on our way through the canyon. There were places in the canyon that widened out to a nice little valley with lots of fresh grass growing up for feed for the horses; also lots of water in a river at the bottom of the canyon. Those sections were a pleasure, and we enjoyed travelling in our covered wagon, but there were other sections of the canyon that were narrow, and the road had to be blasted out of the side of the mountain.

After leaving Conrad, Montana, and driving for a day, we were out in a desolate no man's land. The evening after the day's travel, we camped alongside a milky pothole for the night with no indications of trouble of any kind except the shortage of water. In all that day, we hadn't seen a living thing, and we had the prospect of reaching the Missouri River by the following evening, where we could replenish our water supply. Dad, Mother, and I rolled into our bunks at dusk after securely picketing the horses for the night, and awoke early that morning to get a good start for the river, where we planned to camp that night. You can imagine the disappointment it was for us to find that our horses had been stolen that night, leaving us out in such a desolate country, short of water and on foot, with a food supply running low. Well, Dad started out after breakfast and walked all that day in search of the horses, but returned that night without finding a trace of them. The following day, he started out to walk to a ranch that was about twelve or fifteen miles away to see if he could borrow or rent a saddle horse. The rancher was very obliging and loaned Dad a horse, and the rancher also told Dad that, in those parts, a man had to take the law in his own hands to protect himself and his property. For the next week, Dad scoured that country with a rifle strapped to the saddle.

In all the ten days we were stranded there, only two wagons passed on that trail; one was a sheepherder's chuckwagon that left us what water he could spare; the other was some people travelling north to Alberta to homestead, also. These people stopped for the day to try and help us locate our lost horses, but with no success, they journeyed on. By this time, Dad and the rest of us were pretty discouraged, and Dad thought the only thing we could do was to have what we had hauled someplace and sold for what it would bring, and return back to the city. That was a hard decision to make, and Dad was so determined to win and settle on the homestead that he had filed on in Alberta.

Dad continued the search, and then one day while Dad was still out searching and I was looking for water, a rider rode up on one of our horses and told Mother he had heard that we had lost our horses and that he had found them. Also, he told Mother that if Dad would make it worth his while, he would deliver the horses to our camp. As there was no other alternative, Dad had to deal with the thieves on their terms, although it took most of Dad's cash.

The next day, we got our horses and didn't lose any time getting away from those hellish surroundings, and by nightfall we were camped at the Missouri River, where water never did taste sweeter, even if the river was muddy. Our next stop would be at Shelby, Montana, where we could take on enough supplies to carry us cross-country to Sweetgrass and Coutts on the Canadian border.

Travelling by Scow
to Lloydminster

*This memoir, by Madge Isabel Strong, is particularly interesting in
that she describes how her journey to Lloydminster, Alberta, included
travelling by scow up the North Saskatchewan River in 1903.*[1]
*She also takes time to describe the fast-paced town of Edmonton
that she visited along the way, and the border town of Lloydminster where she eventually resided. It should be noted that she also
mentions an English colony on the western prairies. What she is referring to is the Barr colonists, a group of about two thousand people
from England who settled in the Lloydminster area in 1903.*

■

Early in the year 1903, my parents, who were British, noticed a
write-up in an American newspaper, telling of a group of people in
England planning a colony in western Canada. We had moved from
Ontario twelve years before to live in the United States, and my
mother was especially anxious to have her family back in Canada.
Besides my parents, our family consisted of my two brothers, J.R.
and George H. Scott, and myself, a widow with a small son of one
year old, and as we were all in our early twenties, the idea of pioneering appealed to us, dreaming of a country well laid out by roads
as shown on maps in the Immigration Office. So, after a great deal

of thought and planning, it was decided that my younger brother, George, would start out going to join this colony by a trip to Edmonton, where he would buy lumber and hardware to take where it would surely be needed.

On his arrival, he found that the only way to reach his destination would be by wagon or down the North Saskatchewan River by scows, an almost unheard-of adventure. He spent a few weeks gaining all the knowledge available, and then, with two scow loads of lumber and a few extra men, started on the trip, which, fortunately, was successful. However, on reaching the colony, he found lumber was not nearly so necessary as food, so he, the young doctor, and an older man formed a company, called Hall, Scott and Co., for running a general store. He returned to Edmonton by what was a stage, a two-seated open buggy, and through Mr. H.H. Cooper, a wholesale grocer, obtained the necessary supplies. The first store was in a tent, but before the year was out, they had gathered enough lumber to build a frame one, where, I am told, a community Christmas party was held. Through the summers of 1903, 1904, and 1905, my brother took scow loads of merchandise down the river.

My older brother followed to Lloydminster in the fall of 1903, he having travelled by train to Saskatoon, then walked the rest of the distance as it was too cold to ride on the so-called stage. That winter, my father also journeyed north, but to Edmonton to see what it was all about, as he said, and waited for Mother and me to arrive for the spring's first scow trip.

Early in May 1904, we reached Lethbridge at seven in the evening, from Great Falls, Montana, this being considered the easiest way, and found the small station floor completely covered by men in sheepskin coats, fast asleep or pretending to be, as they waited for transportation to the coal field. I approached the ticket agent, through a door on the platform, to ask if we could get a berth in the sleeping car going through to Fort Macleod on the eleven o'clock train, and he said it was impossible. I then asked where we could wait. He took a look into the waiting room and shrugged his shoulders, so we settled for an old bench on the platform, where I tried to make Mother and my small child comfortable, while I spent most of the time walking back and forth, worrying and wondering why we had attempted such a crazy trip.

Finally, at eleven o'clock, the train from the east came in, and standing at the steps of the sleeping car was the porter and one lone man. I hurried to them and inquired of the porter if it was possible for him to find a place on his car where we could sit the distance to Fort Macleod. While he was shaking his head, the man spoke up and offered his berth, which was not made up. They helped us into the car, where my baby rewarded this gentleman by throwing up on him. However, in a few minutes, he and the porter returned, and he insisted we should leave the arrangements to him for a bedroom over the station, where we would rest until eight o'clock, when we would take the train to Calgary. How he accomplished it, I don't know, but we got the room where we could stretch out for the few remaining hours. I have never forgotten that man and his great kindness, although I forgot to ask his name in my gratitude.

We reached Calgary that day and stayed a few days to rest. Then we boarded the train to Edmonton. There was no hurry in those days, even the train took twelve hours to make the journey, with a stop at Red Deer for lunch. Everyone got off the train and wandered up a slight slope to some frame building, a restaurant, and when the train crew had had enough to eat, the two or three sauntered back to blow blast after blast on the whistle until all passengers returned.

We reached Edmonton in early evening, over the Low Level Bridge to a small station below Bellamy Hill, and were rejoiced to see Father and George waving their Stetson hats to us through the window. The town was small, with its west boundary a little north of the Hudson's Bay store on Fourth Street and the main street called Jasper. When asked how the main street got its name, one would be told the story of a man who, upon reaching the townsite, chose the name because he thought he had reached heaven.[2] The people of the town were certainly not slow, like the train service had been. Everyone seemed keen and so alive, the place seemed to be bursting at the seams.

Our stay was only a short one while the scows were being made ready and laden with supplies, and while waiting, I often took walks, one being about two blocks from Jasper Avenue on First Street, where we picked wild flowers.

▲ Travelling by scow in 1910. *Image PA-3760-124. Courtesy of Glenbow Archives, Archives and Special Collections, University of Calgary.*

Much interest was shown in the scows, which were necessarily well-built and new each trip because there was no return. They were forty feet long, eighteen feet wide, and three feet deep. They were packed solidly and covered by tarpaulins, making it possible to walk over them. The steering was accomplished by what they called sweeps: trimmed trees of a certain size, with one in the centre of the first scow and the second in the centre of the back. They were mounted like oars and handled in the same way, sometimes taking three men for each, the scows being fastened together, and two being the limit to handle.

Our crew consisted of two Indigenous pilots, five young men going to the colony, one being a cook, and my father and brother George. Thus, early one morning when all was ready, we embarked from a short distance west of the Low Level Bridge. Steering the scows between the piers caused some excitement.

Shortly after leaving Edmonton, we were around the first bend of the river and out of sight of any habitation until we reached Lloydminster. The North Saskatchewan River was, and is, a shallow stream, its current swift. It changes in depth according to the season, spring and early summer having the highest water. There are many twists and turns, also quite a few rapids even at its highest, and due to its vagaries, it adds up the mileage. Our trip in May, when the river was high, took seven days, while my brother's last trip that summer, in early September, took six weeks with a few portages.

A small tent had been erected on the first scow for mother, my baby, and me, which was very comfortable, with cots and chairs. The men slept in bedrolls on the second scow and seemed far away at night, when we were anchored to trees on the shore and listened to the howling of coyotes that came as close as they dared.

We were blessed with beautiful weather until the last afternoon, when a violent storm came up, the wind becoming so strong it was necessary to lower the tent, while I sat on the side of mother's cot, holding the canvas up with my head, diverting some of the rain. Aside, though, from that storm, the days passed quickly, gliding between the banks of the river. The trees were beautiful with new green leaves, and the birds sang their best. The only living thing we saw was a big bear, who paid no attention to us as he drank from the river. On the fourth day, in the late afternoon, as we were approaching the biggest rapids, it was decided by the pilots to pull in to shore and wait until morning before attempting them. The next morning, we passed through the rapids, which certainly were formidable, and although it was often frightening, it was most interesting watching the pilots choose the channels by the colour of the water.

Three days later, after the bad storm, late in the afternoon, we arrived at the landing place called Fort Pitt, although there was nothing left of the fort. The shore was flat ground where wagons would approach for loading. My other brother was there with several men and a mounted policeman from Lloydminster. An open, two-seated buggy had been brought to convey mother, me, and my child to the town twenty miles away, where we were welcomed by my brother's friends until we moved into our log house with its sod roof a few days later.

There were a few frame buildings in the town, a bank, general store, and an Immigration Hall, this being built by the government a little late for the newcomers to take advantage of. However, I was told tents had been placed at intervals along the route to be travelled by the colonists, each tent having a cookstove and plenty of wood, all supplied by the government, and probably was of much more comfort than the Immigration Building would have been.

The homes, when we arrived, consisted of a few log ones, tents, and sod houses made of slabs of sod piled one on top of the other, making thick warm walls. The roofs of these houses, log and sod, had sods placed on small bare-tree rafters, and when well-built were waterproof and looked quite well until the grass and weeds sprouted a year or two later.

Surveyors had by this time marked out the streets. The two most used were Church, where the log church was built, and Main, being also the Fourth Meridian, which, when the provincial boundaries were defined in 1905, divided Alberta from Saskatchewan. Living and working in both provinces made no difference, as the town grew rapidly through lumber being hauled in by wagons from Saskatoon and Edmonton. By 1904, when we arrived, things had settled quite well, and the people who had not gone a distance to their homesteads moved back and forth, doing business in the town.

▲ Winter in Lloydminster, Alberta, in 1903. *Image* NA-303-72. *Courtesy of Glenbow Archives, Archives and Special Collections, University of Calgary.*

During my four years in Lloydminster, there were three memorable events which have stayed with me all these years. The first was a prairie fire in late March or early April in 1905, when we had an early dry spring. I am told there were fires the year before when some homesteaders were burnt out, but this I think was the only one that threatened the town. Word had come the night before that, unless the wind changed, it would pass some miles away, but by morning,

all the men were told to hurry to the south to make a fireguard of the two ploughed Sections, where the land between could be burned off, the high wind which had arisen making the situation serious. All day the men worked, beating out the sparks that blew over the fireguard. The people working to save the widest part of the town never thought of the women and children in the narrow part of the town, three or four blocks distance away, and by afternoon we were out also, fighting flying bits of burning grass over the road or trail into town. Fortunately, on the west side, the new railroad grading, which had been done in the summer of 1904, saved us there, but we spent some hours, the few women and larger children, beating out every bit that threatened with wet sacks.

The second event was a joyful one, the coming of the railroad, something the settlers had looked forward to since arriving. Then, one morning in June 1905, we were up early looking for the smoke of the engine. Everyone was excited and up much too soon, but by nine o'clock we could see it, and within not too much longer after, an engine pushing two flatcars—the first car carrying the ties, which were placed by one crew; the second crew following with the rails off the second car. The engine followed, pulling a few more cars, and slowly and surely passed through the town to the happiness of everyone, although it was some months before we had train service, which also changed the close community feeling of the town.

The third event that impressed much on my memory was a typhoid fever epidemic in the fall of 1907. There were only two doctors and one nurse in charge of the hospital available, and although appeals were made to the larger centres for nurses, it was impossible to get help, as typhoid fever was a scourge all over the West in the fall of the years, and 1907 was one of the worst. We had a large number of cases and several deaths, Father being one of them.

Daily Living

*Sylvia Mitchell, writing in the third person, offers a thought-
provoking account of daily life on a homestead in Saskatchewan.*[1] *From
living in a sod shack to planting gardens to discussing prairie fires and
cyclones, she offers a compelling insight into the responsibilities of each
family member and the role each of them played on the family farm.*

■

Warmly the wind came sweeping over the knee-high prairie wool that
stretched away to the far horizon. The sun rose swiftly in an almost
cloudless blue sky. The land was flat like a table, with a faint blue
haze of hills in the distance. The city woman, newly come to this vast
unsettled country in 1907, opened her door.

The home was a small one-roomed sod shack with one window
facing north. The door faced east. Along one wall were two bunk
beds. A table, two kitchen chairs, a rancher cookstove, and packing
cases piled up for cupboards filled the room. Her big square oak table,
the scrolled high-backed chairs, and fine furnishings from the Old
Country were stored in a barn roofed with poplar poles covered with
hay and straw from the first crop. Alas, it leaked and ruined many
prized possessions.

The small window had no curtain, but it needed none, and at
night the lamp on the table shone out across the flat land for many
miles to guide the traveller home. The husband worked in the town

twenty miles away for money to buy their food, and walked home sometimes at the weekend and back again on Sunday night. Once, he mistook a star low on the horizon for the lamp and went towards it until it set. It was only when daylight came that he discovered he was many miles from home.

Near the shack was a slough with rushy banks (a haven for mosquitoes, frogs, and small insects). Here, from a seep well, they got their drinking water. Water for washing was hauled to the door in barrels on a stoneboat when they got oxen and the men were home. Otherwise, the housewife had to lug the pails from the slough herself. It was heated in a copper boiler on the stove. Then she set up her round tub, got out her scrubbing board, and rolled up her sleeves. It was a glorious day when they got a washing machine worked by hand. A clothesline stretched between the house and the little house out back where lay the useful old Eaton's catalogue. Many a prairie child practised his reading while poring over the goodies in that book! In winter, the washing was peeled off the line and came in crackling, stiff as boards, to be set up or draped over chairs beside the stove to thaw out. Snow was gathered too, and melted. It took an awful lot of snow to fill that copper boiler!

Occasional trips to town were made in the lumber wagon with the oxen. It took all day, but was a real treat for the whole family. As money was scarce, however, the two children had to be contented with a bag of hard rock candy. Later on, the frightened city woman learned to milk a cow and harness horses. When a democrat was bought, she even learned to drive. She baked bread now for all the bachelors near them, and made butter with the thick yellow cream she set to rise in the dark cellar.

Large herds of antelope drifted across the horizon. These provided some of their meat. Coyotes, badgers, and jackrabbits were seen. Jackrabbit stew was common and delicious. In the fall, flocks of wild turkeys settled in the grain fields, and geese by the thousands, as well as ducks, passed overhead.

Prairie fires were not uncommon. Started from lightning, careless smoking, campfires, or even sparks from the trains twenty miles away, they destroyed the grazing, and the prairie wool never grew as tall and thick again. The fires also burned the trees for building

▲ A coyote lying in the snow near Beynon, Alberta in 1900. *Image NA-43-250 by H.B. Biggs. Courtesy of Glenbow Archives, Archives and Special Collections, University of Calgary.*

and firewood. The coal, hauled twenty, thirty, or more miles from town, was very expensive. Coal fires were sometimes banked at night, but coal gas was dangerous in the tightly closed houses, so fires were often allowed to go out. In the morning, everything was frozen and the ice had to be broken on the water pails before the kettle could be boiled. Hot stones were wrapped in towels to keep the beds warm. They were also used on the long cold trails to keep the feet warm. One young girl used to carry a hot potato to school in her muff to keep her hands cozy.

One day, there was a prairie fire when the husband was away. The sod shack had a fireguard around it, but the barn did not. The housewife feared the straw barn would be burned as the fire came close, and she went out to fight it. She dressed in her husband's overalls and soaked a heavy skirt in water. Setting her children on the doorstep to call her if she got lost, she went out into the darkness. She fought all night and did get lost, but was guided home by the children calling. She could do no more and they went inside. Then suddenly the wind shifted and the fire swept by a few yards away.

A new wooden frame house and a big barn were built. A water dowser or well-witcher came with his willow triangle to witch for water. He found it near the back door. Neighbours helped to dig and curb the well. Soon a windlass and pail sat on top.

One day there was a cyclone. It passed between the new house and the barn but did no damage. A wagon with three barrels in it stood in the way. The cyclone picked out the middle barrel and dropped it over a nearby fence, then smashed a wooden shack and broke the owner's leg. "There were devils in that wind," said the man.

Shortly after the new house was built, the mother was busy getting a meal when the house started to shake, the pots and pans rattled, and the pictures danced on the walls. She grabbed up her children and ran outdoors. It was a slight earthquake that lasted only a few minutes and did no damage, but gave her quite a fright.

Some winters were worse than others. When a blizzard struck and stock had to be fed, the farmer would tie a binder-twine line between house and barn, or carry a ball of twine and unwind it as he went, to find his way back. One man on his way home from town in a cutter became lost. When his horse gave up, he unhitched it, turned over the cutter, and sheltered underneath among his buffalo robes until morning.

Every family had a garden and grew melons, marrows, and pumpkins as well as potatoes and other root crops, to store in the cellars. The main annoyance was the mosquitoes, and even the men wore mosquito netting over their heads and gloves on their hands. The livestock suffered greatly, and in the evenings, smoke bonfires or smudges were built in the yards for them. Women preserved saskatoons and raspberries, and made jelly and jam from chokecherries, gooseberries, and rhubarb. Some farmers even smoked their own meat. Some made sausages.

Neighbours helped each other in sickness and celebration. There was always one woman who would attend when babies were born, as the nearest doctor was twenty miles away. There were all kinds of social gatherings. Anyone with an organ was popular. Everyone went to the dances in the schoolhouses—even the babies, who slept through it all on the desks along the walls. There was always a fiddler. Dances started early and went on until four or five in the morning. They were held on Fridays (mail day). So when you passed the post office (in the mail carrier's house) on the way, why not rouse him out of bed and get the mail? Some did.

Most people seemed to be honest. No one locked their door. If caught in a storm, anyone could go in, even if the owner was away, help themselves to a meal, stay all night, do no damage, but leave

▼ A photograph of the Johnson Stevenson children taken in Airdrie, Alberta, in 1890. *Image NA-582-2. Courtesy of Glenbow Archives, Archives and Special Collections, University of Calgary.*

⌃ It was important to have a cat or two on the homestead. They kept the rodent population down and also served as companions to children and adults. In this photograph, taken in the early 1890s, note the cat sitting on the table, looking at the family's dinner (a pig's head). *Image ND-37-5. Courtesy of Glenbow Archives, Archives and Special Collections, University of Calgary.*

some payment if he was able. People were concerned for each other and helped when they could.

Pioneer children, too, lived a spartan life. They had a few toys and made their own harmless fun. They swam in the sloughs, explored the coulees. They did not feel they were missing anything. In winter, they skated and slid down hills on scoop shovels when they had no sleighs. They dug tunnels in straw sacks and went rabbit hunting. They read a lot, and old books passed from hand to hand among the children as well as the adults. They went to picnics, baseball games, and dances with their parents. When they played, it was with real enthusiasm.

▲ Children are young as four years old were expected to help with chores around the farm. In this photograph, a young boy, around 10 years old, is sitting on the edge of a wagon waiting for a load of hay. Dated 1914. *Sandra Rollings-Magnusson Collection.*

They had few pets, but dogs and cats had their duties and were treated as part of the family. The cats were nice warm bundles of fur in the children's beds on cold winter nights. The favourite calf or rooster became the winter meat or the Christmas dinner, it was understood.

The children worked almost as hard as their parents. They walked, rode, or drove two, three, or even four miles to school. They helped with all the chores and work on the farm. They learned how to cope with emergencies. The training and hardship made them valuable citizens. They lived long lives and left the country better because they had been there.

Yes, things were different in the old pioneering days. The people seemed different too, and this is how it was.

Never a Dull Moment

Evelyn Slater McLeod offers a unique insight into the homesteading era as she recalls some noteworthy events that occurred in her district of Consort, Alberta,[1] from settlers improving their homes to digging wells to helping distressed horses. She also stresses the importance of children's labour on the farm and how children coped on a daily basis.

■

While our settlement was being established, the railroad was extending its line to the small town of Hardisty, sixty miles northwest of us. This was now the nearest point where building materials and farm supplies could be obtained. Lumber was badly needed for better roofs, and for cribbing so wells could be dug, and many trips were made. It was a four-day journey, necessitating overnight stops at roadhouses. A roadhouse was a night's lodging for profit in some settler's home—where one always faced the hazard of picking up bedbugs and lice. A delousing reception always awaited the traveller upon his return home.

As soon as lumber was available, board roofs were added to the houses. Some of these roofs were made in sections and placed on top of the sod ones. To prevent them from blowing off in a high wind, heavy stones, attached to wires, were laid near the eaves. With these wood roofs, rain barrels could be used to augment the water supply. The use of rain barrels continued even after wells were dug and in use, as the barrels supplied soft water for laundry purposes. During the winter months, housewives obtained their soft water by melting snow in washtubs and boilers on their kitchen stoves.

As settlement progressed, wells were dug. Why the willow branch in the hands of Uncle Wesley turned toward the earth at a certain point I never knew, but it did. I watched it many times. He was the expert and witched most of the neighbourhood wells.

The settlers helped each other in a true community spirit when well-digging began. They were all dug with pick and shovel, and the dirt brought to the surface by windlass. As the shaft deepened, board cribbing was lowered to prevent cave-ins. They went down ninety feet on one farm before striking water. During the digging of our sixty-foot well, wonderment was stirred when small seashells were found many feet down. In all the wells, the water proved to be alkaline, but not harmful and not objectionable to the taste.

Much toil went into making living even tolerable, but there was nothing better to bring submission to these tasks than hearing of someone with greater problems. We were told of a tragedy in a settlement somewhere to the northwest of us. The pioneer family lived in a dugout furnished only with apple crates. Food had run out, and in a cold summer rain, their little girl went to gather whatever the prairie had to offer. She drifted with the wind and was not found for forty-eight hours. There were a few wild mushrooms in her basket, but exposure and starvation had brought death.

By the summer of 1910, there were quite a number of school-aged children in the vicinity, and their elders felt their obligation. Their concern resulted in the Willow Brook School being built that year. The school housed grades one through eight, and for many years it also served as the civic centre and place of worship. Our first teacher was Daniel Day, father of Dr. Arthur Day, who later finished his medical education and returned to spend his lifetime ministering to the needs of nearby settlements and in the town of Consort. In time, those who loved Dr. Day saw a pudgy little man, eyeglasses mended with adhesive tape, carrying a dilapidated medical satchel. During the "dirty thirties," those who benefitted from his skills gave him a dollar if they had it left after feeding their families. He was one of them, and he understood. His devotion to the community was total.

Our school was in close proximity to a coulee, from which good spring water supplied the children's needs. They carried the water in a galvanized pail, where it was placed on a box at the back of the room. A long-handled tin dipper rested in it for use by all the children. Part of the spring was diverted by farmers for livestock watering, and that whole area became a quagmire. On one occasion, a horse bogged down in this morass, and his struggles only sent him deeper. The owner, Eber Waite, had thrown a small lasso, fastened to his saddle horn, around the animal's neck, but under pressure the rope broke. He was frantically trying to find some way to save his horse when a neighbour came by. Like all prudent farmers, he carried a log chain in his wagon. This, they managed to get around the neck of the floundering beast, and other horses pulled him out. It was the school noon hour, and we were all on hand for the excitement.

Another fine family, the Houstons, moved into our area July 6, 1912. James Houston was not a well man at that time. They started their sixty-miles wagon course from Castor, then the nearest rail terminal. He drove a four-ox team, and his wife, Clara (with their three-year-old daughter Jean to care for), handled two half-wild cayuse ponies on the other wagon. Son Stewart, barely a teenager, was of considerable help. A lot was expected of farm children in those days, and they lived up to it.

There have been few cattle drives without cowboys and their mounts, but the Houston cattle were driven the sixty miles by their two oldest daughters—Ethel, age eleven, and Pearl, nine. The drive at first appeared to be more than the girls could cope with, but when a young calf was put into one of the wagons, its mother followed and the other cattle strayed less.

At journey's end, they lived in their tent while a frame shack was thrown together from the small lumber supply on one of the wagons. Mr. Houston's health continued to fail, and he passed away in the winter of 1914. After his death, his indomitable widow, clad in her calico blouse and long full black skirt, was a familiar figure riding the plough in her field and driving four horses.

There was great tranquility in that remote locale. When we were expecting the return of a loved one, occasionally we put an ear to the ground to listen for the sound of horses' hoofs on the hard earth and the distant rumble of the wagon several miles away. Then there were the warm summer evenings when the mosquitoes were unmerciful to man and beast. The welcome sight and smell of a smudge built in the barnyard would bring the cattle running from their pasture to the protection of the smoke that so mercifully wiped from them the grey blanket of tormenting insects.

There weren't many dull moments for the teenagers; they always found some way to improve their lot. Lawrence Slater and Lincoln Akre, about thirteen years of age, set up a telegraph line between their homes via the barbwire fence and sent messages to each other conforming to the prescribed dots and dashes learned from a Morse code book.

Then there were always gophers to catch, which not only was a pastime for all the boys, but brought them money as well. One day, Clarence caught an albino gopher. He skinned it and proudly approached his father, who was drawing water from the well. The albino skin called for some examination on the part of Dad, who accidentally dropped it in their ninety-foot well. It could not be recovered, but they never dared tell Mother. Occasionally, youngsters caught young gophers and kept them for pets. Young crows were common pets for many children—I had one myself. An immature coyote was run down on horseback and kept for a while by the Slater boys, but they finally conceded it couldn't be tamed.

Illness struck at times and was well handled by most families. However, an insidious disease attacked one fine young woman, Esther DeWolfe, who had three small children. My aunt and I stopped by one day to say hello on our way with horse and buggy to pick berries. Esther was seven months pregnant with her fourth child. It was her washday. Two stools, on which were large galvanized tubs, stood in the middle of the room with a kitchen chair beside each. We watched in disbelief as this uncomplaining woman, washing on the washboard, rinsed and wrung garments by hand with one knee on a chair, alternating between the two tubs by the use of her crutch.

A little flurry was put into the rural tranquility by occasional crises. George Stauffer, a somewhat dilatory neighbour, had a matched pair of Clydesdales. One forenoon, George galloped up to the nearest farmhouse on one of them and yelled that its mate had fallen in a well. The horse had been missing a couple of days before he became alarmed, and he had just found it in a twenty-foot well on an abandoned homestead. The horse had gone down, rump first, clear to the bottom. By noon, neighbours had gathered to help and had rigged up a windlass. George went down and attached ropes, and they raised the horse to the surface, but at that point the animal struggled and fell back to the bottom again. A second try got him out, but in bad shape, and he did not live.

A trip back in the summer of 1961 to this Consort district where I grew up stirred many nostalgic memories of fifty years ago, and I felt some should be preserved on paper before they were completely erased by time. New frontiers have all but disappeared, and that mode of life on the Alberta plains is no more. To some who have never broken prairie sod, these memories will give a brief insight into the past.

Flour Sacks, Mice, and Rain

*Gladys Marie Kennedy recounts her family's ten-day journey
by horse and sleigh to Grande Prairie to homestead in the winter of 1913.[1] She also remembers building and living in a sod and
log home, using flour sacks as window coverings, experiencing
mice falling through the roof, and coping with rain and heat.*

■

In 1911, I met Norman Hugh Moon. We were married quietly on
March 9, 1912, by Reverend Myres in a Presbyterian church in
Edmonton, Alberta. That fall, Norman and a few men, some of them
relatives, drove with horses and wagons to Morinville, Alberta, north-
west of Edmonton, and on to Athabasca. They continued from the
north side of the Athabasca River to Lesser Slave Lake and Grouard,
where there was a mission, hotel, hospital, then on to Peace River to
Dunvegan Crossing. They crossed by ferry over the mighty Peace
River and on to Grande Prairie. This was around a four-hundred-mile
trip and took around twenty days with horses. They had lots of food
for the men and horses.

After the men filed on homesteads in Grande Prairie, they went
east about eighteen miles to a district later known as Glen Leslie,
where a post office and store were established later, and then on six
miles further east to Bezanson district, where the homesteads were.
Glen Leslie district was named after the storekeeper, and Bezanson

after A.M. Bezanson, who founded it. The men went to the bush and got out green logs for the walls and green poplar poles for the roof to put up a house on Grandma Moon's quarter. They returned to Edmonton another way via what was then known as the Edson Trail.

On February 1913, a caravan of flat racks on sleighs left Edmonton by train to Edson, Alberta, then over the Edson Trail to Sturgeon Lake and finally to Bezanson. This trip took ten days or so, having to travel in winter when the creeks and rivers were frozen. On the Edson Trail we stopped each night at stopping places. We had our own food, and one flat rack was fixed up as a caboose. It had a floor and wooden sides around thirty inches high. A tent was fastened on top of the sidewalls. There was a small four-lid stove in it, well fastened down, a couch for Grandma to sleep on, and a three-quarter-size mattress on the floor. It was fastened up to the sidewall in the daytime. The men slept in the stopping place bunkhouses. We all ate in the caboose, some outside when the weather permitted. We had lots of food and used to cook up a big pot of potatoes, and made biscuits at the stopping places to help the bread supply out.

Going down the steep hills, you had to put what was called a rough lock on the rear runners of the sleighs. This was to keep the sleighs from going too fast and pushing the horses. The horses were well shod, with steel shoes properly shaped by a blacksmith to fit their hooves. What was called corks were added to the shoe. These corks were pointed, sharp steel to prevent slipping on ice and to give a better grip, especially when a load was going up or down a hill.

It was a big day when we arrived at the log cabin, our new home. For a few days, we were all in Grandma's log house while logs, poles, etc., were taken out of the bush to build the other cabins. The house was made of green spruce logs with green poplar poles for the gable-type roof. These were covered with hay the men had cut with a scythe in the fall of 1912. They put earth on top of the hay to fill in the cracks. With the rain, the grass grew quite tall and had to be cut in case of fire from the tin stovepipes; sparks sometimes went right up from the stove. The odd wildflower sometimes grew at first, and even the occasional bird's nest was built. When it rained hard, the roof leaked and dripped for a day or two afterward, so we had to put buckets to catch the drips, and even had to move the beds sometimes. The frost that thawed out the green poles on the roof also made it leak in February, after the heat got going. The heat also brought big bubbles of pitch out of the sidewall logs. They were not peeled and were dust collectors.

Grandma Moon and I slept together; we had beds in the equipment. On one of those leaky occasions, she said to me, "It's a good thing it isn't the house that makes the home, but the love that lives inside."

The windows were holes left in the logs. As there was no glass brought in, flour sacks were bleached to get the writing off, then dipped in melted parawax, which came in pound blocks about the size of a pound of butter, only there were four sections to the pound. These waxed flour sacks were fastened over the holes; they let the light in but you couldn't see out.

If we ran out of coal oil and candles before the men went out for the year's supplies, we made what was called, in Gaelic, a croostin. (Grandma could speak Gaelic.) To make a croostin (apologies to the Scots if this is spelled wrong), you took a large, flat pearl bone button and tied a square of white cotton, around five inches, with a string close to the button so the corners stuck up. You used a metal or tin bowl, put melted fat in it, dipped the cotton corners in it, then put the whole thing in the bowl, corners up and lighted it. You couldn't read by it, just enough light to see your way around. It was real smelly and sooty but served a purpose.

Field mice, of course, built their nests in the hay on the roof, and one day when Grandma was sick in bed, a whole family of newborn baby mice fell through the hay onto her bed. I was there with her so soon did away with the little things. It saved catching them in traps later to keep them out of our food supply. Everything had to be tightly covered and traps set all the time. The flour and white and brown sugar were in hundred-pound sacks; rice, tapioca, salt, etc., in smaller sacks; and, of course, the large cartons of matches were kept in tin pails with lids. One night, Dad and I heard a terrible noise in our first tent-like cabin. A mouse had just got his tail in the trap and was parading around, trying to find a hole big enough to let him and the trap out. Finally, he got away, leaving part of his tail in the trap.

Later on, a log house was built to replace the lumber one, the lumber one being used for the roof of the log house. It was all one room with beds curtained off. I remember one time, it rained hard for days. We piled the food and the baby's and our clothes on top of the trunks, using slickers (men's heavy yellow raincoats) to keep them dry. We put a large table oilcloth over the cheesecloth bed canopy, and anchored it to the old-fashioned bedposts. Pockets of water collected at the foot, it being a lot lower than the head, so we took turns getting up to dip the water out. It was Norm's turn, and he got lazy, so pushed it up with his feet. Of course, that broke the strings and let all the water come in the bed. We had to move to Pete Moon's house, which had a much steeper pitch on the roof, heavier sods, and more earth on top, which held out the rain. Norm, baby Hughie, and I stayed there until our place dried out after the dripping stopped, and we got the mess cleaned up. The water ran into the cracks and soaked away. The stovetop, being iron, had to have the rust scoured off, after it was lit. It took two or three days for things to dry out.

> Many staple products were sold in sacks to the homesteaders. *Image NC-2-398 by British and Colonial Photographic Company. Courtesy of Glenbow Archives, Archives and Special Collections, University of Calgary.*

THE
LETHBRIDGE
ROLLER MILLS
24 LBS.
PRIDE OF ALBERTA
PATENT
THE TAYLOR
MILLING & ELEVATOR CO.
LIMITED
LETHBRIDGE, ALBERTA.

Cattle Ranching

*In this memoir, William Colby Reesor describes his life living on a ranch,
rounding up cattle on the wide open spaces before homesteaders moved
into the area.[1] He highlights the cowboy life—the branding and dipping
of the cattle and the constant surveillance for wolves in the area. He also
details a devastating snowstorm that killed most of his family's livestock.*

Early in May 1903, Dad went east to bring back stock for the ranch.
These eastern animals, usually two years old, were called dogies, a
term applied to all animals and humans who were not range broken.
Included in the bunch he brought back were four carloads, eighty
head for his own apart from the ranching company. We branded
these animals on the nineteenth of May. The date is memorable
because that day the famous May storm started. I believe from what
I have read from the history of the West that the only other compar-
able storm was back in the 1880s. It was a Saturday and my first
branding, and I believe possibly the first time our own registered
brand Bar M5 was used.

The animals, of course, were turned loose as soon as branded. It
started to rain before we were finished, and by dark this had turned to
sleet and snow. Sunday morning broke to a raging blizzard, and this
kept on without let-up through Sunday, Monday, Tuesday, and Wednesday was clear in the morning. The coulees were drifted almost

TOP Two men burying dead cattle that had died in a spring blizzard. *Image NA-2245-1. Courtesy of Glenbow Archives, Archives and Special Collections, University of Calgary.*

BOTTOM Branding cattle in a corral at Jumping Pound Ranch, Alberta, in 1890. *Image NA-1939-3 by S.A. Smyth. Courtesy of Glenbow Archives, Archives and Special Collections, University of Calgary.*

Sandra Rollings-Magnusson

level, with huge drifts around the buildings. The storm started in again after noon Wednesday and kept on till Friday night.

During this time, the men had difficulty getting to the barn to feed the horses and milk the cows. There being no fences, the cattle simply drifted with the storm, and many thousands throughout the country piled up in drifts in the coulees and were smothered. What made matters worse was the fact that many young calves were arriving, and we found many calves, newly born, curled up on top of the snow, with the mother out of sight or almost so, dead. The result was that Dad lost every one of the eighty we had branded the week before. So his start in ranching was disastrous to say the least.

Scotty Gowre, an ex-Mountie to the west of us, who ran a herd of about fifteen hundred head, rounded up less than three hundred. Battle Creek was clear of ice before the storm, but the snow and sleet formed on the surface with the result that stock tried to cross, only to go through and be drowned. I remember my brother Bruce, with others, spending many hours with a team and chain, hauling these dead animals out of the creek, as in many places the bodies had literally formed a dam.

Another interesting phase of ranch life during the first few years was the dipping of the cattle. Stock in those years suffered from mange, and all animals had to be treated. The ranchers got together and built dipping vats at different points, and cowboys from the different ranches would ride together in the roundup, which, of course, was complete with cook wagon and extra horses for the riders. They gathered all animals, no matter who owned them. These vats were located so that each one of them would handle two to three thousand head. I cannot give details as to the construction, but I do recall the vat itself was a trench dug five or six feet deep and maybe four to five feet across. Some of these were long enough so that the animals, when prodded along the chute leading from the holding pen, would either jump or drop off into the five- or six-foot mixture of lime and sulphur and have to swim to the other end, where there was a ramp where they could walk up into a dripping pen. The surplus mixture would then be returned to the vat.

The second type was a cage supported by a block and tackle and a team of horses. Each time the cage was filled, the team would back up, thus lowering the cage. One man would always sit on the fence above the vat with a long, forked pole. Any animals who would not go completely out of sight would be pushed under. Two other men would be on the fence, one on either side of the dripping pen, to record the brands, which were plainly visible when the animals were wet. The dip itself was kept warm or hot by an upright tank at the side with a fire under it, with pipes to circulate the mixture. You can imagine the fun we youngsters had, first in riding and helping to collect the herd on the last day of the roundup, and then, no doubt, making a nuisance of ourselves during the dipping operation.

I think that at this point I should mention the various incidents in regard to the wolves. It is my understanding that the type of wolf found in considerable numbers in the Cypress Hills in those days was not the big, almost black wolf of the far north, but was a breed considerably larger than the coyote and certainly quite capable of killing cattle, although such killings were confined to the young animals, or the old and weak animals in the spring of the year. I might inject here that Mother, Harry, and I witnessed one such killing. One morning when Dad, Bruce, and Frank were away, we heard these animals bawling, or bellering would be the better word, and on rushing outside were just in time to see the yearling come in sight over a small knoll, possibly two or three hundred yards away, and the wolf right behind him. It grabbed the animal by the tendon in the hind leg and, of course, with this tendon severed, the animal was helpless. Wolves apparently seldom kill near their dens, as frequently we would see the tracks in the snow in the morning, right through our herd, and find out later that they had killed at another ranch some six or eight miles farther north.

Later, when we had moved up to the present location of the Reesor Ranch, and for some three or four years after that, a pair of wolves had their den under the rocks on the brow of the hills to the east of the ranch, and on many occasions we would see the pups out playing while the father would keep watch on the top of the rocks where the grass would be worn right down from his pacing back and forth. If anyone appeared, he would take off and keep appearing a short distance ahead to lead you from the young ones. I might add that this is a common practice among both birds and animals.

Another wolf story which might be of interest took place before we moved to the hills. Whether this was the spring of 1903 or '04, I cannot be sure. The weather had turned warm and, as usual, we had closed the gate of the shed, and the cattle had then bedded down on the bare knolls just by the shed. I should say here that Dad had brought a large dinner bell from Ontario and had hung this bell high between two poles by the log house. Of course, there was the usual rope hanging so that we would ring the bell whenever required. Now, about the wolves. One night, before we went to bed, we heard the cattle bawling, and on Dad going to the front door to see what the trouble was, he could see all the cattle rounded up by the wolves running around and snapping at them. Dad took the rifle and fired two or three shots into the air. Immediately, the wolves left and all was quiet. Mother stayed up for a little while after the rest of us had gone to bed, when the same thing happened all over again. Instead of waking Dad, Mother went out and rang the bell. This did the trick. In fact, it stampeded both the wolves and the herd, and we rounded them up the next day some three miles west.

It might appear so far that we were completely isolated. This was not so. Actually very few days went by before cowboys from other ranches, out riding, would be in for dinner or overnight. At the same time, Bruce or Frank would, at many times, be away at another ranch. There being no fences, a continual check on the stock was necessary. Every rider made a mental note of branded animals far from home and passed on the information as soon as possible.

In 1905 or '06, settlers were coming in and homesteaded in the district. Many of these were from the United States. From this time on, living in the open prairies changed, as all homesteads were fenced and land was ploughed and wheat fields appeared.

It might appear to the people reading this story that we boys had a very monotonous life. How wrong you are! I just wish my grandchildren could spend even one of those wonderful years as we did, doing our regular chores both inside and outside, our own saddle ponies to ride to and from school, and during the holidays just going wherever we wanted to, seeing nature as few are privileged to see it today. Getting up in the morning in the winter to see the prairie chickens by the hundreds streaming out of the trees to the south to feed on the berries in the coulees to the north and flying back at night, first into the trees and then simply closing their wings, diving headfirst into the snow to be buried until spring. Or to watch the prairie chickens dance in the spring. The same ground would be used for these dances year after year. One such dance ground was about half a mile north of the house. Whether they use the same spot today, I do not know. The sharptails are few and far between, but hopefully will survive.

The Homesteader
and the Teacher

*Lena May Purdy recalls her experiences of travelling west and
meeting the Purdy brothers, who homesteaded at Boggy Creek,
Saskatchewan.[1] As a schoolteacher, employed to work one
season at the local schoolhouse, she boarded with a married
Purdy brother. Over time, she met and married one of his bachelor brothers, Russel Purdy, and became a homesteader's wife.
In this memoir, she highlights her homesteading experiences.*

I would like to tell something about my husband's homesteading. He
came to Regina, April 1, 1883, with his father and several brothers.
They brought a carload of farm equipment from Ontario. Their father
had been out in 1882 and had chosen a homestead near Boggy Creek.
The day they arrived with their stock, there was still heavy snow on
the ground, and they had some very hard days unloading and taking
several horses and cows the twelve or fourteen miles to the homestead. As soon as they could, the brothers entered for homesteads
and pre-emptions. Will Purdy located on the south side of Boggy
Creek, and Herb Purdy took a homestead in the Tregarva area. For
several years, they shared the teams and implements. The father and
mother stayed only a few years; then they returned to Ontario.

In 1886, the first severe drought struck and there was little crop. Russel Purdy went to Lethbridge, where the government was building a jail and some other buildings, and he got work as a carpenter there. To save all he could, he took his own bedding, and as soon as a building was enclosed, he made a bed on shavings. He brought a nice bit of cash home in the spring and bought cattle. Will had cared for the horses through the winter and, of course, had a share of the cattle.

Russel built only a shack on his homestead, and the brothers built a small warm house on Will's homestead with a small cellar under it. From the first, they made a garden and raised ordinary vegetables, and the bachelors baked good bread and even pies, and picked and canned wild fruit. They let calves run with the cows in the summer, but in the fall and winter they milked the cows and made the best butter, which they sold to private customers in Regina. They kept a few hens, and a sow or two, so had pork to cure for their own butchering.

An older brother, Walter Purdy, built a good pole-and-straw stable on the side of the creek valley, partly dug out of the slope. They had several pretty good mares and raised a few colts. Russel lived on his homestead in the summer and worked the land. He had a small stable there, enough for the horses he used. The Purdys never used oxen. I think he often spent the weekend at Will's place, probably did his baking and washing there, as I am almost certain he had not many conveniences on his own place.

When they got the cattle in the spring of 1887, they fenced the pre-emption quarter of Will's place. There were many springs of good water along the south bank, so there was always water for the stock.

There was plenty of wood in those days in the Wascana Valley only a few miles away, so fuel cost only the labour of cutting and hauling. They worked in this way, making some small improvements, more granaries, a summer kitchen at the back of Will's little house, a better pigpen, gradually bringing more of the land under cultivation.

Their mother came from Ontario a few times and mended their bedding, footed their home-knit socks, and generally put things straight. More families came in and a school district, Boggy Creek, S.D. No. 64, was organized, a schoolhouse built. The school, during the early years, was open only in summer.

▲ A woman schoolteacher riding a horse to the schoolhouse in the Boundary Creek district of Alberta in 1901. *Image NA-2443-1. Courtesy of Glenbow Archives, Archives and Special Collections, University of Calgary.*

In 1895, by a rather strange sequence of events, almost accidents, I was engaged to teach there for the summer. My home at Cottonwood was not very far from Boggy Creek, and I knew many of the people in the neighbourhood as we often met at picnics and the special church affairs. I was sent to board at Walter Purdy's, the married brother. I spent a busy, pleasant season teaching the school and taking part in Sunday school, attending church services held in the schoolhouse, acting on committees for picnics, and such things. In the fall, when the school closed, I went home, thinking I would study for a higher certificate.

But instead, in 1896, I returned to Boggy Creek as Mrs. Russel Purdy. I found the house improved, a new floor laid, a brick chimney built, a well dug by the back door, and a shed built over it, and in the evening, we drove to my new home. I found that Will, who was to live with us for a while (we went to his house), had baked a big batch of excellent bread and several pies, the house was clean, stove polished, lamp gleaming. Oh, but that was a cold day! November 24, forty degrees below, air milky, windy, drifted snow into the trail so the fine team of drivers could not get up any speed.

Eventually, Russel sold his homestead near Tregarva and bought Will's homestead. Both had title to their homesteads. Will went back to Ontario.

We started the next spring to plant shelterbelts and shrubs. My aunt in Ontario sent me cuttings of red and white currants and gooseberries, and they grew well. We had very fine rhubarb old Mr. Purdy brought from Ontario in 1883, and the bachelors had planted asparagus. We planted raspberries, and a few years later, Mr. Dobbin in Regina got me strawberry plants from near Collingwood. We covered them in winter and they did moderately well.

My husband, like everyone else, had grown Red Fife wheat, and in the early years of that century, people began trying earlier varieties. We waited till Marquis was pretty well-tested, then switched to it.

After marriage, we made butter all the years, selling butter, eggs, and, in the fall, pork to our regular customers in Regina. We supplied several of them with potatoes too, and after, sold them rhubarb.

We always calculated to pay all household and living expenses with the cows, chickens, pigs, a young horse or two to sell every year, two or three beefs, fattened to sell between the winter-fed cattle and the fall grass-fed, and the bits we sold from the garden, so our grain income could pay a man's wages and go for improvements. We had made a good beginning at raising registered Clyde horses.

Every year we made some improvements, fencing one year all around the cropped quarter. One year, we built a fine, big barn and a stone stable in place of the pole-and-straw stable. We built a fine concrete house in 1903 and had six children by 1908.

Then in 1910, my husband was not well. He got what seemed like a good offer for the farm, stock, and implements, and we sold and moved into Regina.

The West Is No Place for
a Loafer or a Kicker

*In this memoir, Mabel Hawthorne describes the hard work associ-
ated with daily life on the prairies, and at the same time highlights
her appreciation for the homesteading life.[1] From living in a sod
shack to feeding a threshing gang to boarding a teacher (who served
and died in the First World War), Mabel comments on the mental
and physical strength needed to survive and carry on with life.*

We found out there was lots to be learned about building sod houses.
We built our own, by our own plans, which we enjoyed for four years.
After a couple of years, you had to renew the roofs or they would leak
when it rained, which made it necessary to keep an umbrella handy
beside the bed if it stormed in the night. What I liked most about a sod
house was you couldn't hear the wind, of which there is always plenty
on the prairies, or the thunderstorms I always dreaded. But it was all
new to us, and we felt it was all a great adventure, never to be forgotten. We were young, with most of our lives ahead of us, and with our
sod house we enjoyed many a hilarious time that first winter, which
seemed to pass quickly. Then we would be going home, which was a
grand and glorious feeling. That was the foundation which made the
pioneer glory in his lot when his natural comforts were fewer and his

⌃ A homesteader standing in front of his soddie (a house built of rect-
angular sod strips) in 1906. *Image S-B1061. Courtesy of Provincial Archives
of Saskatchewan.*

wealth not much greater. Our homes were truly homes, even if only
a two- or three-room sod shack, as it was in the early days, to shelter
us from the burning sun and the howling blizzard. We found a sod
house warm in winter and cool in summer.

It was amusing at times to hear the children of the different homes
comparing each other's houses. One would remind the other that
theirs was better because it had a floor in it, and the other would say
theirs was better because there were little trees growing up all over
the floor and they could dig wells in it.

We got from three to five meals a day, and an occasional letter and
the latest paper, from two weeks to a month old, with the great big
hope of a wonderful future of seas of golden grain and the network
of railways, gave us strength to overcome the unsurmountable bar-
riers in making a home, which called forth every ounce of physical
strength we had to give. How did we do it? Baking dozens of loaves
of bread, making our own butter, caring for chickens and turkeys,
tending gardens, milking cows, making our own soap, pickling our
own pork for smoking, canning and preserving under almost primitive conditions, and doing our own sewing for our family didn't leave
much time for dreaming, and yet the dreams were there engrossed

in our homes. We accepted all that went with it. But always dreaming of better days to come.

For over two years, our nearest post office was Saskatoon, sixty miles by trail, and we just had to take chances on getting our mail through our neighbours and friends. Of course, our neighbours extended to thirty miles around. When one brought the mail, he would generally have mail for everybody on the trail as far as he went, and would bring in the bag and empty the contents on the floor so each one could sort out their own and return the remainder into the bag, and the traveller would wend his way down the long, long trail a-winding, with a team of oxen as it generally happened to be. And oh, those letters! Did we not appreciate them? How we did enjoy a letter from home, and a plum pudding at Christmas, and many other goodies which helped to brighten the days of the lonely bachelors and homesteaders.

In this West, everything is intense, even the weather. We can say we have the coldest climate, the hottest, the windiest, and even the most glorious sunsets to be seen anywhere. To most people, the West is most strenuous. There were fewer solid comforts in 1905 and 1906. The West is no place for a loafer or a kicker. In a county so vast and open, it was not easy. The true westerner was a big-hearted, big-souled, "glad to meet you, what can I do for you" sort of man. And he had no time or patience for such tales as "we do this or that better in the East, the US, or the Old Country." But in cases where a helping hand was needed, the hand was there.

One great attraction was the strong bond of common interest, which held the community together: The crop question first and foremost, and still is, as it furnishes the livelihood of the country, the comforts of the human element. The crop is the whole concern, yet should the crop fail, he is loath to admit it and says it might be worse and is quite confident that next year will be better. It has always been a great "next year" country, and although we have had our bad years, along with good ones, it is our heritage. Saskatchewan has earned the title of being the wheat province and bread basket of the world. Until a man has stood in the month of August and gazed over the great plains, and has seen, as far as the eye can see, the nodding heads of wheat ripple and roll like the endless waves of a golden sea, as,

NO 5

▼ A threshing crew on a farm south of Wauchope, Saskatchewan, in 1914.
Image R-A12371. Courtesy of Provincial Archives of Saskatchewan.

until 1927, stooks dotted the plain from horizon to horizon, he has not known the full charm of the Canadian west.

Since the combine has come into its own, it is wonderful to see these huge machines, both binder and thresher in one, especially at night when they travel all lit up. You would think it was a travelling village on wheels when you scan the neighbourhood far and near. We looked forward to the threshers coming. When we heard the machine was in the neighbourhood, we always knew when our turn would come, so we got stocked up, dozens of doughnuts, pies, cookies, and loaves of homemade bread. Eggs were preserved in waterglass weeks ahead, and pickles of all descriptions were made in advance. Also, for meat, a pig was generally butchered and fried down or roasted in its own fat and would keep for months. A couple of days before threshing day were spent mainly in cooking, with a huge fire in the old-fashioned range, while the tempting odours caused the children to come in after school hopefully remarking that they were "awful" hungry.

The vegetables also were prepared and left covered in cold water, and ready to put on to boil at a minute's notice. Also the woodpile was prepared by the chore boy, who always remarked, "I hate to cut up a lot of wood as you will only burn it!" But when the hungry men came in to the well-laden table, that was all forgotten. When we had the table set and all was ready, I would meditate a few minutes to see if I had forgotten anything, then would breathe a prayer that tomorrow would be fine, for should we have a spell of hot weather, all our precious food would spoil and all our work would be in vain. In 1920, when they threshed a few hours, it started to rain and not a wheel was turned for three weeks. As long as we used our neighbours' teams it wasn't so bad, as they just took their horses home and started to fall plough or other fall work. But when the cook cars came into being, we didn't have the gang to feed, but we sure had lots of horses to feed. Those Ontario fellows had no worries, only to get in a good fall and get home again with their loot, and the horses they were driving from far and wide got fattened up, to be turned out to stand the strenuous winters on the prairies. When we couldn't thresh, we sometimes would take a load of wheat into Harris, as that was our nearest town, for a neighbour when we had to go in, so we didn't go in empty. And the neighbour would return the compliment when he got threshed.

On one occasion, I had to go into town for repairs and took in a load of wheat for my neighbour. Jack, Miss Campbell, and my two boys, Wallace and Perley (six and eleven years old, respectively), came along for company. All went well until two miles north of where Harris is, and where the old stopping place and post office was. It started to sprinkle, then pour, and rained for three days. However, I got my load off at the elevator, then got half a ton of coal, as wood was soaked now. So the elevator man and Ed Cram helped me and hurried me on my way homeward, nine miles northwest, as soon as possible. And just as we were crossing the railroad track, the iron on the neck yoke fell off right on the track, and the train was coming.

Jack Turvey was at the coal-shed door and saw what happened, and in a jiffy, with his hammer in hand, put it back on, and we got off the track just in time to let the train go by, which was a long freight. We had a big strong team of horses which never seemed to tire, but when we got to Eagle Creek it was tough going, but they made it, and when we got to Albert Crawley's, Mrs. Crawley was at the road with coats and nice lunch for the boys, as it was very hot on leaving home, and we didn't take coats along. There was no time for treats of any kind around Harris; our only hope was to get home in safety, which we did, and the girls had a good, hot supper ready for us. And when we got our wet clothes changed, the water was running out of our boots. So all was well, and no one was any the worse, a good coal fire fixed everything, and the horses got an extra bite of oats for their part.

Hillview School was built in 1906 and opened by our first teacher, Ivan Tinkness, on March 1, 1907. As I remember, the school wasn't opened on schedule, as Ivan had the misfortune to freeze his feet badly going to the bush for wood, and even when he did come to teach, he could not get a shoe on for months. Ivan taught there for about a couple of years and boarded with us in the soddie. Which I used to say was our own little pile of mud.

Ivan's home was Anglia, Saskatchewan, where he homesteaded along with his father and mother, also a sister and brother. They originally came from Ontario. He joined up with the Princess Pats early in the First World War,[2] and he was later transferred to the 12th Battalion, with which unit he entered the trenches. Later that winter, he was seriously wounded by a shrapnel explosion and lay buried for hours under a pile of debris. He was finally dug out, more dead than alive, and after a long period in hospital returned to Saskatoon. Later, having recovered from the effects of his wounds, he re-enlisted for active service with the 183rd Battalion and was granted a commission. Word was received by his sister by a cablegram on February 11, 1916, that Lieutenant Ivan W. Tinkness of the 183rd Orange Battalion had died of wounds received in fighting on the Western Front. This was the first fatality in our district, as we all claimed Ivan and he was much loved by everyone here.

When a man has stayed, say, two years in the West, and having inhaled the pure, sweet air of the prairies, and seen the broad hills, lakes, and winding creeks, and the magnificent wildflowers, he will seldom wish to leave it, or, leaving it, he will long for it ever, as a sailor for the sea.

Why do we have this longing? One reason is the people in the older places are settled into their groove and fixed in a certain position and station in life, and they are expected to live and die in that station. In the new country, there are greater opportunities for progress and betterment as broad as the prairies, and advancement is only limited by incapacity to take advantage of them.

All Gone into the Dust of Time

In this memoir, Joan S. Phelps discusses her Welsh family herit-
age and tells the tale of her family's accomplishments of travelling
from Wales to Saskatchewan to homestead.[1] Her story is one of
heartbreak and sorrow as family members passed away.

His name was Thomas Davies. It is written that he was born on November 16, 1851, in Waendilan, Nantglyn, Denbighshire, in a small stone cottage overlooking the Vale of Clywd in Wales. In the churchyard of Nantglyn are large slate slabs inscribed with the names of his Davies family in a direct line as far back as 1693.

The Davies men were farmers, sawyers, and furniture makers—strong and brave men. Thomas was known to walk long miles over the rugged mountains of north Wales. One of his sons described him as virile, fearless, and proud, as well as very loving, tender, and kind. He had the "Welsh spirit" and a temper as well. Those yet living who remember him say, "Boy, could he swear!" Perhaps he had to for the sake of survival.

Just before he was eighteen years old, Thomas married a widow with two children. He and Hanna then went through five births of their own. Their child number five was stillborn, at which time Hanna went Home to be with the Lord also. Thomas took a second wife, this time a widow with four children. Eight of the children between them were under ten years of age. Thomas Davies and Ann Jones, in the years to follow, produced eight births. The first was stillborn, but the other seven lived and were deeply loved, even to my generation. In 1904, this large Welsh family migrated to Saskatchewan, Canada, as homesteaders. Six months later, Ann died at the age of fifty-two, and Thomas was alone once more with many children.

Meanwhile, another Welsh family had left the homeland and gone to Patagonia. John Jenkins had married Johanna Davies, and they had seven children, some born in Wales, some in Patagonia. Johanna was born on March 13, 1864, somewhere near Cardiff, perhaps in the area of Tylorstown or Ferndale, South Wales. It was said of her that she was gentle, kind, hospitable, social, a wonderful mother who raised her children with the Bible.

On June 29, 1902, Johanna and John Jenkins, with their seven children, left Patagonia with a group of other Welsh families to pioneer the settlement of Llewelyn, Saskatchewan, as homesteaders. It was near the tiny town of Bangor that John Jenkins was killed during the building of a barn on his Canadian farm. The main beam fell on him.

Johanna Jenkins and Thomas Davies, both alone now, with children and homestead farms near Bangor, were married about the year 1907 and lived in a crude log cabin on the Davies farm. The barn was unique in that it was dug into the side of a hill there in the Qu'Appelle Valley of the prairie, where spacious flatness prevails. The indentation of it, scarring the gentle slope now covered by a wheat field, and half of a crumbled foundation to a home, with a hole in the ground that was the well, are the ghostly remains of the farm today.

October 8, 1909. Thomas was fifty-eight years of age and Johanna was forty-five years. My mother, Margaret Ellen Davies (aka Peggy), arrived in the crude log home on the prairie. She was the last child either of her parents was to bring into the world, but not the last Thomas would be a father to.

Eight happy years followed for Peggy Davies, in spite of the poverty and hardships of homestead life on the prairie. The family was large and loving. Everyone came for tea, for overnights, for longer. Tiny Peggy, heiress to the Welsh spirit, stamped her wee feet at a vole in the dooryard and told it to "Go home." She would accept the dare from the other children to pilfer the sugar lumps from the pocket of Mrs. Pant Mawr when she came for tea. She remembered the Sweet Williams in Johanna's vegetable garden, the only flowers a busy farm wife had time for. Picking wild prairie flowers, saskatoons, and wild medicinal herbs were also pleasures for her. So were the quiet times when Johanna read the Bible to Thomas, who could neither read nor write, and also taught the Scriptures to Peggy.

September 1917 brought tragedy again. Johanna rose early, and while she was lighting the kitchen stove with coal oil, there was an explosion which ignited her flannel nightgown. Her burns were extensive. Young Peggy gave her sips of tea as she lay in agony, dying. Then the gallant Welsh lady was gently put in the back of a grain wagon and taken five miles into Bangor, there to be put on the train for the fourteen-mile trip to the Melville Hospital. Within hours, she passed into eternity.

Two years later, bereaved Thomas took his Peggy and returned home to Wales, to Blaenau Ffestiniog, to work in the slate quarry and to marry wife number four, Mrs. Dancy, a widow with four children. In 1941, Thomas died a quiet, natural death kneeling by his bed one morning.

Peggy herself became an immigrant when her brother brought her to New York City, grown and ready to work. She went to Utica, New York, to visit another brother, met my father, D. Robert Simmonds, and married him in May of 1930. She was killed in Greens, New York, on August 1, 1974, in an auto crash.

They are all gone—all gone into the dust of time. There are so very many of my generation scattered across the US and Canada. Some of us keep the lines of communication open with the love of family, our Welsh heritage, and our belief in the Scriptures.

The Great Blast of a Cyclone

*In this memoir, G.F. Gudmundson offers insight into the tragedy
and hardship his family experienced after a cyclone destroyed
their Saskatchewan farm.[1] While he describes the death of
his mother and the injuries sustained by his other family
members, he also tells of neighbours and friends who immediately came to their aid. He describes the assistance of the doctors,
and the help they received from the community of Elfros.*

■

Cyclones are rare on the prairies, but occasionally one strikes, and
when it does, the results can be devastating. I know, because I was in
the middle of one.

A cyclone struck our Saskatchewan farm home at midday on
June 19, 1927. Today, the memory of that awful event is as keen as
though it happened yesterday.

Our home was left a burning wreck. My mother was killed; my
sister, out from Winnipeg on a holiday, was seriously injured; my
brother had body lacerations and a multiple-fractured leg; and two
other members of the family and a visiting guest had minor injuries.
Yet, so completely was our little home devastated that it was incred-
ible anyone escaped alive. In the case of my father, particularly, it
seemed that a miracle happened. Blind and in poor health, he was
resting on a couch in the front room, talking with our guest, when the

cyclone struck. After, when neighbours came to our aid, they found him under the upturned cot, twenty feet from the wrecked house and unhurt.

The cyclone came with such a speedy onrush that even if there had been an adequate shelter available, none of us could have reached it in time. It had been a hot, sultry morning, with an ominous, oppressive feeling in the air. We noticed the massing of dark storm clouds in the west and expected an electrical storm.

Then came the cyclone. It touched the ground about a mile to the west of us, at a distance from any buildings. It cut a swath through the wooded area, went over and down a hill, then raced on to our farmstead on the bank of a coulee.

My first sensation was of a great blast coupled with a terrifying darkness. It seemed that I was again on the battlefield and that a 9.2 had burst over me,[2] and I felt that this was "it." Then came a blackout. I came to, and saw our nearest neighbour, Able Gielson, bending over the body of my mother, muttering and glancing around with a bewildered look. Rain was coming down like a cloudburst—this, I suppose, is what revived me—and continued for half an hour. Then the sun shone again.

The house—a three-room dwelling—the barn, granaries, and all other buildings were torn to smithereens. The house was burning—probably set on fire from the cookstove. Wreckage was scattered like driftwood over the countryside. Even now, we occasionally find splinters here and there, or a battered kitchen utensil miles away down the coulee bank. Our farm machinery—a binder, seed drill, and other implements—were carried away and twisted so badly they could never be used again. Yet a supply of sawed wood which my father had neatly piled about ten feet away from the house was undisturbed, and milk pails placed on the wood pile to dry in the sun were still in place.

And now, the neighbours began to arrive from every direction, in spite of almost impassable roads, and by horse and wagon. All possible help came, one felt, right from the hearts of the people.

➤ A cyclone near Vulcan, Alberta, in 1927. *Image* NA-1416-14 *by McDermid Photo Laboratories. Courtesy of Glenbow Archives, Archives and Special Collections, University of Calgary.*

▲ Mrs. C. Bull sitting in her sod home in McLaughlin, Alberta, after a cyclone in 1900. *Image NA-1662-5. Courtesy of Glenbow Archives, Archives and Special Collections, University of Calgary.*

A first aid centre was set up in the community hall in Elfros, some five miles away. Dr. Palson and Dr. Cumberland were there and soon were joined by other doctors from adjacent areas. Water was heated, dry clothing provided, cots and bedding set up. Most welcome was the feeling of genuine compassion and personal warmth from all around us. And it didn't end there. Later, the whole community got together and made the most generous contributions, enabling us to establish ourselves again.

Though, in truth, it is one of the hardest things in life for one who is independent by nature to accept charity, even when it is tendered with love. Yet if you assert your independence, you merely satisfy your pride by refusing the helping hand of a brother. It gave me comfort to feel that through an active and useful life, I could in some small measure compensate the community for what they had done for us.

It was no easy task to get us to Elfros over water-soaked roads. Put to the test of ploughing through ruts, over bumps and mudholes, the Model T gave a performance that would put modern cars to shame.

My sister hovered for days between life and death. She had apparently been knocked unconscious, and lay in the smouldering debris of our home until help came. She had deep, extensive burns over her arms, legs, and back. There were no wonder drugs in those days. Dr. Palson decided that an intravenous injection of a saline solution was an essential emergency treatment. But the materials had to be obtained at the Eyolfson Pharmacy in Wynyard, sixteen miles away over formidable roads. My friend Malcolm Aird immediately volunteered to make the trip in his Model T, returned in record time, and the transfusion was successfully made. As soon as my sister could be moved, Dr. Palson and his good and gracious wife took her to their home and with diligence and love nursed her back to recovery. About two months later, she took her first steps again.

On my cot in the Elfros Hall, I learned what I feared—that Mother had died. It was a dark hour.

My mother had the best qualities of the early settlers. She was courageous and resourceful, and though outspoken and apparently stern at times, at heart she was gentle and understanding. Of unquestionable honesty, she could never tolerate any duplicity. She was an Old Country–trained midwife, and in her homeland had braved the elements by day and night, on foot, on horseback, or in a small open boat, sometimes trudging over mountain trails, sometimes crossing an angry fjord. In the early days of Saskatchewan, when doctors were at few and distant centres, she thought nothing of going out in thirty-below weather, with a stiff northwester blowing, to help a woman in labour.

Now she was gone to her reward, but her memory is a blessed one.

The Fury of the Wind and
the Blinding Snow

*Albert Elderton was a bachelor who decided to help out friends
who were picking up a load of coal from Swift Current.[1] While the
trip started out pleasantly enough, the group soon found themselves in the midst of a terrible blizzard. This memoir recounts
how they made their way back home in howling winds, blowing
snow, and temperatures of minus forty degrees Fahrenheit.*

On Boxing Day in 1911, Jimmy Wilson, Bill Gibson, and myself, A.E.
(Bert) Elderton, left Jim's place in the Kyleville district by team and
wagon to go to Swift Current, between forty-five and fifty miles away,
to get a load of coal. The weather was nice, but there was snow on
the ground. We went by wagon because Jimmy had no sleigh, and he
intended to buy one in Swift. Arriving there, Jimmy found there was
not a new sleigh in Swift to be bought. We waited in Swift two days
until a sleigh was shipped from Moose Jaw. Then the next day, we
put a load of coal on the sleigh and, leaving the wagon in Swift to be
picked up later on, we headed for home.

It was a most lovely day, and so warm that we had even taken off
our coats and walked along beside the sleigh in our shirt sleeves as
we laughed and sang, told jokes, and whistled away the time, just like

happy, healthy, young homesteaders. Then, almost without warning, the sky clouded over rapidly, and soon we were driving right into the teeth of a howling, raging blizzard, with the temperature dropping rapidly. We had left home without much real winter clothing, probably because we didn't have any.

The storm caught us about ten miles out from Swift. There were very few habitations on the old Battleford Trail in those days. The storm got so bad, we could not ride on the sleigh but had to walk alongside in order to keep warm. Thus we slogged it out for another twelve miles until we came to what was known as the 8-Mile Coulee (meaning eight miles from the South Saskatchewan River ferry crossing at Sask Landing). Here, a Mr. Miller lived with his family. He had room in his house for us and room in the barn for the team. The Millers made us very welcome and treated us with that true spirit of western hospitality so prevalent in those days. Warm and cozy, we spent a happy evening with the Millers while the storm raged on outside.

After a restful night, we awoke to hear the storm still howling, and after breakfast our host remarked, "Well, I guess you won't be tackling it today, eh?" But Jimmy was anxious to get the coal home and, being mindful of the family at home, eager to get started. Bill and I, with the spunkiness of youth, figured we could make it. Even when we had the team harnessed and were all ready to hitch up, Mr. Miller came out and begged and pleaded with us to put the team back in the barn, saying, "There will be better days than this, boys," and telling us about how he once got out in a storm while a cowboy around Calgary and came nigh to freezing to death. But all in vain. Jim and I figured we had been away from home long enough, and Jim kept wondering more and more how the family would be making out.

So out into the storm we trudged. We had only gone a few miles when we wished we hadn't started out. The storm was so fierce, and the deepening and drifting snow made the going pretty heavy for the toiling team. They got a little relief when we came to the river hills, as it was downhill for a mile or two and a gradual drop of 410 feet from the top of the hills to the river level. We could have stayed at the old stone house built by the pioneer Mr. Goodwin on the river flats, but as we had only gone eight miles or so from Millers, perhaps we reckoned it would be sissy to quit at that little distance. So on we went over the river ice. Climbing the long north hill, the faithful team straining every muscle to lift that load another four hundred feet up to the top of the hill a mile or two away, we felt the same as the horses; we had our mettle tested too.

The fury of the wind and the blinding snow was so strong that, again, we could not sit on the sleigh to drive, but had to walk and drive at the same time. It was strenuous work, stumbling through the snow, trying to steer the horses along the almost obliterated trail while keeping the head turned sideways to avoid the flying snow from stinging the eyes so hurtfully. It tired a man out before very long. So we had to take it in turns. One would drive while the other two dropped back and got what shelter they could by crouching behind the sleigh. When the driver got tired (which did not take very long), one of us would move up ahead to relieve him, and he would move back, and when the second one got tired, the third one would take his turn at it. Thus, we struggled on for another four miles to Mr. David McCrie's place, he being one of the first settlers to take up land north of the river.

Mr. McCrie had built a house and barn, but the house was abandoned for the winter while Mr. McCrie and his wife had gone on a trip to their old home in Ontario. Feed had been stacked at the barn, so we put the horses in and fed them. We managed to get into the house, and as there was a stove there and we had coal on the sleigh, it would have been "duck soup" for us to have stayed for the night. Unfortunate for us, though, was the discovery that, just like Old Mother Hubbard's, the cupboards were as bare as a newborn baby.[2] Obviously it would have been silly to go to Ontario and leave goods in the house to spoil. And we were three very hungry young men to whom the appeal of food was more enticing than the calculated risk of the wintry spaces.

The team being rested, we decided to push on to the Larsens' place, four miles up the trail. It was still tough going, even for a team that was fed and rested. When we got to Ed's place, we found his little stable full of stock and his little house full of family. Even if we could stay in the house, we certainly could not let the team stand out all that stormy night. One thing was certain: the team had had enough

A Travelling from place to place in the winter meant that people were reliant on horses and sleighs. Dated 1914. *Sandra Rollings-Magnusson Collection.*

of that load for that day. However, we decided to try for Josh Turner's house two miles farther on. "Come, cheer up, lads. 'Tis to warmth, food, and shelter we steer," and we were on our way. We were happy when we got to Josh's, and Josh and family were happy to take us into their little wooden shack. They had room for the team, too, in the stable. Mrs. Josh kindly attended to our creature comforts, bless her dear, departed soul, and we three slept side by side on the little shack floor. It wasn't the "Bessborough,"[3] but it suited us, right down to the ground floor, so to speak.

I have said the weather was cold. Next morning, Josh's son, Bert, went out to the stable to milk the cow, said stable being composed of rows of poles driven into the ground three feet apart, and the space between packed tight with straw. Soon Bert was back saying, "I can't get a drop out of her. Her teats are frozen." We had no thermometer, but we felt it was anywhere from forty to fifty degrees below zero. Fortunately, the storm had abated, and bidding our hosts a very good, warm "Good-day," we hit the trail for Jimmy's place, another six or seven miles.

This was New Year's Day, and somewhere around noon we reached Jimmy's to find "All's well," with still enough fuel on hand and a bang-up turkey-with-all-the-trimmings dinner, already put on the table. I feel sure that was once in my life when I went from the ridiculous to the sublime. Jim's wife, Josie, was an excellent cook (as us bachelor boys in some mysterious manner soon found out). So, six days after we had started out, we were right back where we started from.

Nipper Saved Our Lives

Robert Wood tells the story of how he and his brother set out on a trek to find some missing cattle in the winter of 1899.[1] Trying to survive freezing temperatures and illness, the two of them finally made their way back home, to the great relief of their family members. Their five-day experience on the cold prairie terrain is laid out in detail by Robert.

In the fall of the year 1899, having finished a season of teaching at Kinistino School, I was helping to do the chores on my father's rented farm, on which he had a small store. My father at that time owned a herd of cattle numbering about 110 head. As hay was getting scarce in the vicinity, my brother Jim had started a ranch at Leather River, about fourteen miles east of the store. During the summer and fall of 1899, he had been erecting the necessary buildings on it and putting up hay. The herd of cattle had also been taken out there so that they could be kept under observation. That whole country was at that time a wilderness, and with only two squatters on it—two brothers named McDonald.

About the end of September, just as things were getting in shape on the ranch, the whole herd of cattle disappeared, and the most intense searching failed to locate them. The search was finally halted till the first snowfall should come so that we could track them. That fall was a very fine one, and it kept fairly mild up till

New Year. Then we had our first snowfall—about five inches—and my brother Jim and I decided that it was time to renew the search for the cattle.

Preparations were made, and my mother cooked enough food to do us for a week. The weather had continued mild up till then, but the day before we had planned to start, it turned very cold. As everything was ready, however, we decided to go anyway, and in spite of the morning of our departure being colder still, we started off. We took a good team of horses, a sleigh, a deep wagon box, oats for the horses, and, best of all, a good riding horse, a stallion named Nipper. And it was this riding horse that, I believe, eventually saved our lives, as the story will show.

Starting out on a morning of the first week of January, we got to Carrot River that night, a distance of about fifteen miles, and camped there. We lit a good fire, had our supper, and then went to sleep, or tried to sleep, in the wagon box. We spent a very cold night, you may be sure, and never camped that way again. The next day we made another fifteen miles or so, going northeasterly along the course of the Carrot River, and this day, one of us rode Nipper and ranged far and wide on the east bank. That night we camped in a dry poplar bluff, and profiting by our experience of the night before, we turned the deep wagon box on its side, lit a twelve-foot fire in front of it, and took three- or four-hour shifts of sleeping there, the one on duty piling wood on the fire as needed.

In this way, though the weather was much colder than it had been the previous day, we got through that night without almost freezing to death, as we had the first night. The third day was a repetition of the second. One of us drove the team northeasterly, following in a general way the course of the Carrot River. But we got no trace of the cattle. The fourth day we kept on the same general direction, and that night when we camped, we estimated we might be forty or forty-five miles from home.

The weather had been getting steadily colder since we left home, and on the morning of the fifth day we decided we had gone as far as we could with the team. However, we decided we would make one last cast with the riding horse, and in the grey of that morning, Jim left on Nipper, going northeast, while I stayed in camp and chopped down dry poplar most of the day, cutting it into twelve-foot lengths. I would say that our camp was about half a mile from the river.

It was intensely cold, and when darkness came that night and Jim hadn't got back, I became very anxious. We had a shotgun with us and about a dozen shells. An hour or so after dark, I fired a shot, and thereafter, every half hour or thereabouts, I would fire another. In that time, I went through all the emotions of the condemned man who was to be executed the next morning, for I had made up my mind that Jim was frozen, and I had no intention of going back without him. But about nine o'clock that night, Jim rode into the camp.

He had a remarkable tale to tell over the campfire. Travelling northeast in the morning for quite a few miles, he had stumbled upon an Indigenous camp. After Jim explained himself in some way and managed to inform them that he was looking for a band of cattle, the Indigenous people, some of whom apparently knew a few words of English, told him that the cattle were safe and were only a few miles from their camp. The absence of snow had helped them and they were coming through all right.

Jim did not go any further, but late that afternoon took to the bed of the Carrot River, heading southwest towards our camp. After travelling slowly for hours, and for long after dark, he had no idea whether he had passed the camp or was still approaching it. He had his heavy fur coat on and the collar up over his ears and could not hear anything. Suddenly, he saw Nipper prick his ears and knew he must have heard something. Scrambling up the steep bank at the first feasible place, he gave Nipper his head and the horse walked back about a mile and some distance from the river and finally walked into the camp. He had heard one of my shots in the first place, no doubt, and had then located the camp by the smell of the campfire. It was a very tense moment for both of us. If Nipper had not heard that shot, Jim would have been completely lost and would no doubt have frozen, as he had no way of making a fire. The temperature that night, ascertained by us when we finally got home again, was sixty-four degrees below zero.

That night, Jim became very ill, and in the morning I had a sick man on my hands. I knew it was going to be a close thing. I decided my best chance would be to try and locate the Leather River Ranch, which would be, I thought, about thirty miles south of our camp. Fortunately, the sun was shining the next morning or I would have been lost in a very short time so far as going south was concerned. With Jim lying in the bottom of the sleigh and almost everything I had piled on top of him, I travelled steadily south all that day. There could be no stopping. Darkness came and I then used the stars to guide me. Then, on the snow, I found a faint sleigh trail. How it had come there, I did not know. As it seemed to be going south, it might lead to the ranch, but I had no idea as to this.

I had to take a chance. Jim was still lying flat on the bottom of the wagon box. I put the reins in his hands and told him I was riding ahead, but I doubt if he understood me. I slung the axe in my belt, swung on Nipper, and made the race of my life for about two miles, following the faint trail. I rode finally into the yard of the Leather River Ranch. I put Nipper into one of the open stables and tore into wood chopping for some stove wood, working like a fiend. There was a stove in the shack, with a stovepipe going outside through the wall and protected by some tin.

I had a nice fire going when the team walked into the yard. They had been able to follow the trail in the same way, though in the dark it was hardly discernible. I dragged Jim out of the wagon box the best way I could, dragged him into the shack, and put him close to the stove. I then stabled the team, and the rest of the night kept the stove red hot, Jim lying propped up beside it and covered with blankets. The log shack was unchinked, and it was naturally impossible to get it warm, but you could partly take the chill off, and it was heaven compared to the outside.

There was no sleep that night. In the morning, as soon as daylight had appeared and we had had something to eat, I hitched up the team, and Jim, with my help, managed to stagger to the sleigh. I covered him up, tied Nipper behind, and headed west for the remaining fourteen miles home. I drove into the home yard that afternoon with Jim still alive, and I would say that in a few days he was all right again. My mother had been almost out of her mind. Five settlers, headed by Jim Cameron, a close friend, had organized a search party that would search for the bodies of the "Wood boys" as soon as the weather moderated a little. But none of them ever dreamed they would see us alive again.

The sequel to all this happened about a month afterwards, when the weather had considerably moderated. Then my brother Jim, accompanied by a settler named Jack Beddome, rode to the Indigenous encampment, and Jim found the cattle a few miles away. They then drove them back to the Leather River Ranch. Out of the 110 head, only one cow was lost, and so my father escaped what would have been a serious financial loss.

Lack of Medical Help

R.R. Knight remembers some of the hunting experiences he had, with his first two stories being humorous adventures, while his third sets a more serious tone.[1] Relating his own personal experience of being shot and suffering, Knight is very forthright in his opinion regarding the lack of medical care available during the homesteading era.

I had a shotgun and I loved to hunt. And on the first Sunday morning that I was in this country, I got it under my arm and took a walk, thinking of some of those mallard drakes that I had seen around the sloughs. I heard a loud "Quack, quack, quack" in a certain direction on the other side of the bushes, so I got down on my hands and knees and finally on my stomach, crawling up in order that I might get a view of these ducks on the slough. For some mysterious reason, as I approached the slough, the quacking suddenly stopped. This I couldn't fathom, and I thought that they must have flown without me seeing them. In the distance again, there was this "Quack, quack, quack," so I proceeded to crawl another half mile, and there again, as I approached the slough, the quacking stopped. And then, suddenly, the idea occurred to me that there was something other than the duck that was making the noise. Afterwards, of course, I discovered that I had been in the pursuit of frogs.

Another time, I had taken my gun and gone down toward Goose Lake. Going along the little path among some scrub, I suddenly saw a black and white animal such as I had never seen before. And very foolishly and innocently, I took a shot at it and killed it. I went up to it and picked it up by the tail and discovered that it was probably a skunk. I threw it aside and thought no more about it and, strange to say, didn't even notice any odour, but the climax came when I reached the farmhouse door where I was working at that particular time. When I went to the door, the lady came rushing at me from the kitchen and said, "Have you been in contact with a skunk?"

I said, "I don't know, but I shot one, at least I think it was a skunk."

Well, after that she closed the door in my face, and a long stream of underclothes, shirts, and trousers came out the door, and she said, "You go down to the bar and get into the trough, and get yourself bathed well all over and then change into those clothes," and that I did. That was my first contact with a skunk of the four-legged variety.

Once, in the fall, I had an interesting and what might have been pretty tragic experience when moose hunting. We had two companions who had gone up to Witchekan Lake, and there I had an unfortunate accident and was shot through the neck by a bullet from a .44 Winchester. This occurred, I would estimate, about seventy miles from the nearest medical help. That would be seventy miles away at North Battleford. There was no snow that fall, and we were returning home with the moose meat in the wagon box. We had stopped for noon when this accident happened. There's no need to go into detail how it happened. But the fact was that the bullet went through my neck. It scraped the spine closely enough so that some chips of bone came out of the wound. I was told later by the doctor that the jugular vein had been laid bare but not touched by the bullet in its transit.

The job, of course, was to get me to help. There was no way to go, and we were there in the bush. There was no road. There was what they called a cut-out, which was a passage cut through the bush by the surveyors, and some people had been using it for a road—a winding affair around the stumps. As I say, there was no snow that fall. Actually, the hunting had been good, and therefore we had a wagon instead of a sleigh. And even people who don't know much about such conditions would realize that a wagon over a frozen muskeg was a rather uncomfortable outfit to be riding in.

I fell in the bottom of the wagon box when I was shot and thought at first that I didn't have long to live because of the quantity of blood that seemed to be coming from down in my chest. However, I persisted in living, much to my surprise and my companions', who asked me if there was anything that they could do! Well, I didn't know what to do. We all had long beards, we were in a state of dirtiness, I'm afraid, from lack of attention. We'd been in the bush for three weeks. Our towels, such as we had, were all filthy. All I could think of was that the boys should tear a piece off one of those dirty towels and poke a piece of material into the holes at each side. Well, they did that and they said, "Well, there's only one thing that we can do and that's start for home." So away we went in this jolting, bumping wagon, jolting along and, every once in a while, banging on a stump.

Strange to say, the bleeding did stop. In fact, I'd never expected that it would. And when I realized I was going to live, the shock made me almost, I don't know the word. They tell me that I talked and talked and talked about everything under the sun. After some hours of this torture, we got to the first shack in the bush near civilization. The boys carried me out. There was nobody at home, but we didn't pay any attention to that. The doors were always open. We went in, and there was an old couch thing that somebody had slept on. They laid me on it, and one of them started for town. Our own team was played out, so my friend scouted about, and within a mile or two he found a stable where there was a team of horses. Again, the owners were not there, but he took the team, hitched up the sleigh and headed for North Battleford.

Later on, I heard that after quite a time this team played out too, and when he got down to the country where there were good prairie trails—no built roads, remember; simply the wagon tracks—he got a bicycle from another man and proceeded from there, and so he went by team and by bicycle until he finally reached help. The doctor did not reach me until well on in the afternoon of the next day, so I imagine it was thirty hours at least since I'd been hurt. I don't know whether it's fair to the medical profession to tell the rest of this little story, but I think it should be done because it does show somewhat of the conditions under which we lived in those days.

▲ Most doctors, in the early years, travelled by horse and wagon or buggy. When vehicles became available and roads were built for traffic, it is likely that doctors travelled in vehicles similar to the one in this photograph. This was the first vehicle driven in Medicine Hat, Alberta, in 1905 and was owned by Dr. C.F. Smith. *Image NA-1824-1. Courtesy of Glenbow Archives, Archives and Special Collections, University of Calgary.*

The doctor had a car. There were very few cars, but the doctor had a car, and he was only able to come about forty miles from town, and then he could come no further with the car because the roads wouldn't permit it. But a man whom I knew, who had a democrat and a team, offered to bring him on up into the bush and see if they could locate the shack where I was resting.

As I say, he finally did reach there, and when he came into the house, he didn't come to me, he didn't look at me. The friend who had stayed with me greeted him, and the doctor washed his hands, in preparation for looking after me, I suppose, and then he said, "Well, who is this fellow anyway?" I did look pretty disreputable. I expect I was pretty dirty. I had this beard and all the rest of it, but what the doctor was worrying about was when he was going to get his money.

He wanted to know if I was a charity case or if there was any council to pay my bill. And he pointed out that his expenses were pretty serious, because he had to come all the way to this house, forty miles out in his car. My friend with the democrat, of course, wouldn't charge anything.

Well, my own father had been a doctor. My father was a man who didn't charge many patients, certainly never charged the poor ones anything. I think he was bound up in what good he could do for people in treating them. Of course, that's by the way. This particular doctor we're talking about asked my friend these questions. So my friend said, "Well, I don't know. He's a young Irish fellow. He's got a homestead out here. I don't know anything about how he's fixed." The doctor said, "Well, go ask him." So my friend came over to me and told me. And in view of my background and in view of what I considered rather an ill-advised time to be talking about money, as I was lying there not knowing whether I was going to be dead the next day or that day, I said, "Tell him I haven't got a damn cent!" Which is what my friend told him.

This wasn't exactly true because I had been threshing that fall, and I had accumulated quite a little roll. As a matter of fact, I had two hundred dollars sewn up in my shirt. We had to sew money in our hunting shirt pockets. I wasn't going to leave the money in the shack while I'd be gone for weeks. However, the doctor finally got around to me. There was nothing he could actually do. He gave me a shot of morphine, and I was loaded in the democrat and off we went on our long drive to where we got the doctor's car. We got down there sometime in the night, and from there we went on down to the Notre Dame Hospital in North Battleford, and there I was for two or three weeks.

Fortunately, there was no hemorrhage or infection, and the wound healed up very nicely. I suppose, since I've told you about the doctor demanding money, you wonder if I ever paid him. [When I was out of the hospital,] I handed him his fee in cash. That's the last I ever saw of him.

I think I should tell you how vital the matter of good health was under the conditions in which I was living at that time. You will realize that with the long distances from the railroad, it was extremely difficult to get medical help of any kind. But there was more in it than that. These people were not able to pay for the medical attention that they should have had. One must remember that these people had no capital. Oh, they had a cow or two, and an axe and a team, and maybe a walking plough and a sleigh and so forth. But when they came up against real medical expense, it was just hopeless. And even at the prices which doctors and hospitals charged in those days—and they were much less than they are now—even then a person who was sick was faced with an almost impossible situation. If he couldn't get it done on the basis of charity, then he couldn't get it done at all. Because these people were very reluctant to mortgage, shall we say, their whole economic future on account of a doctor bill or a hospital bill—they would take a chance. And many a person during the homesteading period in the north was buried who should not have been buried at all, because if he had had proper attention, he would have lived.

Prairie Fire and Desolation

In this biography, Dorothy Gush recounts her family's initial experiences on the prairie after they had travelled from England to Saskatchewan in 1905.[1] She tells of how they built fireguards and fought prairie fires, broke ice in the winter in order to water the stock, and travelled sixty miles to pick up supplies from the nearest town. While she emphasizes the difficulties associated with homesteading life, she also tells of beautiful summer days and her encounters with friendly wild animals.

In November and December of 1904, my father was very ill. The specialist told him he would probably not pull through another winter in England and advised him to move to another climate and live an outdoor life. If he followed this advice, he might live for many more years. We left Newbury early in the spring of 1905, my father and mother, sister Annie, aged twenty-five, and I, who was sixteen, leaving my married sister Flo in England. My brother had previously moved to western Canada.

My brother and Sid Purdue [a friend] were at Lipton, Saskatchewan, to meet us, each with a team and wagon. The furniture had not arrived, but fortunately we had several large boxes of clothing and blankets with us. These were loaded into the wagons along with the groceries we purchased. Poor Mother was advised to take enough groceries to do for several months, and to her amazement found herself ordering two hundred pounds of flour, a hundred pounds each of white and brown sugar, several twenty-pound pails of lard, pounds and pounds of raisins, dried apples, peaches, and prunes, as well as soap and many other things.

We arrived in a real prairie wind, dust flying everywhere and even tin cans being blown off the town dump. I remember one of them hitting me on the leg as we struggled across the street to the hotel. My brother told us we would have to stay at the hotel a day and a night to give him and his friend time to take the first load home and then come back for us. They would sleep under their wagons at night, he said.

When we were ready to start out, we hired a democrat from the livery barn, whose owner was to drive us. We set out early in the morning with our tobacco-chewing driver. He made his living in those days by driving settlers to find their land and, of course, stabling their horses when they came to Lipton. He did a really good business. There were no roads, nothing to guide us but these heaps of earth. Every few miles, our driver would stop, get down and spit on these plates, grab a handful of prairie grass, and rub hard to get the dirt off so he could read the figures—all a very mysterious procedure to us, of course. This went on all day, and he continually bragged that he never got lost. It got dusk, and he had to admit that he had lost his bearings. He drove to the top of a slight rise and then told us we were in luck; he saw smoke and it meant a settler. So off we went in the direction of the smoke. It was so dark by then that he couldn't see anything, and he kept muttering something about the North Star.

Presently, something that looked like a large mound of earth loomed ahead of us. It was a sod building, and the smoke was coming from a pipe through the roof at one end. There were no windows and only a dark opening for a door. A very scared-looking woman looked out. She turned out to be an English person whose husband had succumbed to the land urge and took a homestead. She had two small children, and her husband had gone to Lipton with the team of oxen to get supplies, a trip that would take four days. The poor soul! When she saw my mother, she burst into tears of joy to see another woman.

By dawn, we were ready to start on our way. Mrs. James made us promise to come again, which we were able to do in the future since we later discovered our place was only ten miles away—very close in those days.

What a shock when we first saw our new home! It looked to us like a toolshed, but at least it had windows and a door, and when we realized that my brother had hauled all of the lumber, nails, tarpaper, and windows all those sixty miles, we realized how hard he had worked and began to really appreciate how well he had done. Our driver only stayed long enough to have a meal with us. Then he was off again back to Lipton.

There were no partitions in the house, but luckily, having plenty of blankets, they served our purpose. My brother slept in a tent outside, and we divided the house into three rooms—the largest room for the kitchen, and two others for bedrooms. Prairie grass with blankets over it on the floor were our beds for six weeks until our furniture arrived in Lipton. My father and brother, and some hired help to get our furniture moved out, made the trip to Lipton, and at that time we got our first mail. The men could not spare the time to make this trip often, because there was the house to finish, a barn to build, and hay to cut and store, besides the required acres to plough, though my father was able to hire some help from Lipton to do his share of the work. The oxen were used for ploughing, and while they were slow, they thrived well on the prairie grass, where the horses needed oats when they were working, and these oats, too, had to be hauled the sixty miles.

Mash had to be hauled in for the cows and hens, but in return we had plenty of milk, cream, and eggs. We could have had plenty of pheasant, partridge, and rabbit, but no one had the heart to kill them. They were all so tame, all the birds and small animals. They had no fear of us, just curious as to what sort of animals we were. I spent many happy hours that spring and summer. In the spring, the mother animals, foxes, wolves, badgers, and skunks, would play with their young families all around me as I sat on the grass, even running over my feet. Even the wolves were quite friendly, and gophers and chipmunks were everywhere, running over me and tugging on my hair as I lay on the grass.

Our first big excitement after our arrival was experiencing a prairie fire, the largest we were ever to see. My father and brother had gone to Lipton for a load of lumber, as we were getting ready to build onto our home in the spring, so my mother, sister, and I were alone. We had, of course, a fireguard ploughed around our house, barn, and haystacks—a strip of sod turned over, about twelve or fourteen feet wide. That was one of the first things we had been advised to do when we arrived.

Just about dusk we could see a red glow in the sky away over the hill, and our hearts went into our boots. A prairie fire! I, being the youngest and a bit of a tomboy, climbed to the top of the house to try to see over the hill. What I saw was flames and smoke far, far away. But it seemed no time until the flames were licking the hilltop. In the meantime, Mother and my sister had brought all the clothes and blankets they could onto the guard. I had to get the cows and oxen, which were tethered for the night, onto the guard, where I staked them very short. They kept sniffing and became more and more excited, and I was worried for fear they would panic altogether, pull the stakes out, and take off. I kept talking to them and patting them.

As the fire got very close to us, it seemed that it must jump the guard. It was fierce and very frightening, and the roar of it was like an express train. I guess we were all praying very hard, and I always said it was a miracle that, as the fire passed us, it slowed down and seemed to die out, then flared up and raced on as fast as before. It travelled sixty miles an hour. I know that, because it reached Lipton exactly one hour after it passed us, and that was sixty miles away. My father and brother arrived home at four in the morning in a light rig they had hired in Lipton, the horses white with foam. They were sure we had not survived, and how thankful they were to find everything safe.

I will never forget the desolation when the daylight came—black everywhere, just black earth as far as one could see. But saddest for us was that our pasture for the animals was gone. Some of the bluffs were still burning. We were lucky that our haystacks had been saved and we had put up lots of it, and I do mean "we," for I had learned to pitch and stack hay that summer. Why the sparks from the raging fire did not carry over to our stacks of hay, we will never know.

Another thing I will always remember of that awful night was seeing a band of wild horses silhouetted against the skyline in the flow of the fire as they knowingly stood for safety on the fireguard my brother had ploughed on his land atop a hill right opposite our house, snorting and pawing in their terror. I have never seen anything to equal that sight since.

Our first winter was a real experience—no plumbing or water in the house. Holes had to be chopped in the ice each day, and the animals taken from the stable to the slough. Then freezing in the cold while waiting for them to take their leisurely drink. The cows were strictly my responsibility, and I had to hurry them along, leading them by ropes. If they did not move briskly, their udders were liable to become frostbitten, which caused them pain when we milked them. Many a pail of milk was kicked over.

When the slough froze to the bottom, it meant watering them at the well. We had been lucky in striking a good well the first summer, but in winter it meant pulling up water in buckets with a rope, hand over hand. The rope soon became like a huge icicle, making it very difficult. At the same time, one had to be wary of being butted into the well by an impatient animal. When the water in the well began to get low, it meant bringing in large tubs, which were placed behind the stove and filled with chunks of ice chopped out of the slough. We poured boiling water over them and carried the water in buckets back to the barn. This was not just the first winter, but went on for several years. How we longed for spring.

I think that it was about our third year here that the Grand Trunk Railway had reached a point six miles from our farm. Once the railway came, little prairie towns sprang up, seemingly overnight. Our nearest one was Raymore, just six miles away, and the nearest town we ever had. These small towns all had the usual church, hotel, lumberyard, livery barn, grain elevator, and general store and post office combined.

The threshing of the grain in the first years was quite an event. Our first crop was threshed by a man who owned a large steam outfit and travelled around from farm to farm. The wheat straw was burned to heat the engine. They usually backed a hayrack, drawn by two oxen, up under the blower where the straw came out, and the poor beasts were just about buried in straw; just their heads would be sticking out. When the rack was full, they pulled it around to the firebox, and another team took the vacated place under the blower. That went on

▼ A farmer working in his field with his stooks of wheat, in 1910. *Image PA-3828-1. Courtesy of Glenbow Archives, Archives and Special Collections, University of Calgary.*

all day, two men stoking the fire while others gathered the stooks of grain and brought them to the machine. If you were the last to get threshed, then the sheaves had to be stacked and were threshed from the stacks. Often, the last farmer on the route was doing it with snow on the ground.

Up to twenty to twenty-five men were in the threshing gangs. It was indeed a hectic time for the farmer's wife. They were long and hard days, and how those men could eat! We had to be up by four in the morning to prepare breakfast for the men so that they could get to work at daybreak. If it rained while they were with us, they had to wait and we had to feed them. I remember keeping them a full week one year, because of bad weather. Feeding the men and oxen all that time took a very large slice out of the crop money. No eight-hour day for them when they did the work, either. Dawn to dark was the rule, and even after dark by the light of a burning straw stack. Later on, when our crops were larger, neighbours were also closer, and the women used to help each other at threshing time, coming to stay as long as the gang worked a farm.

After supper, the farmer had his own chores to do, cows to milk, and horses to water, feed, rub down, and bed for the night. At our place, I milked the cows, filled the mangers with hay, filled the oat boxes, and threw straw into the stalls for the night.

Coal-oil lamps were our only source of light. One good thing about the oil lamps was that, as long as we kept them filled, the light never went off. They were smoky things, and the lamp globes got very smoked up. Newspaper was used to clean them when we could get it, but in those days, newspaper was a scarce article. Keeping the wicks trimmed reduced the smoke somewhat. The stable lantern was even more of a smoker and gave a very poor light. The first winter, it was very spooky to go into the sod barn after dark to do the milking and hear the muskrats scuttle away amongst the straw as one opened the door. I did lots of singing in the dark to keep my courage up. The cows loved to be sung to while they were being milked. They were not a bit fussy about the calibre of the voice.

When more land was broken by incoming settlers, the prairie fires became less frequent, but there were still some. We sometimes had to backfire them or beat them out with wet sacks and so save the pasture land. One fire got into a corner of our crop. The men were away fighting a fire on the other side of our farm. Prairie fires have a nasty habit of producing a thin line of fire, which would break away unnoticed and later build up into a big fire some distance away. This had happened to us, and it was up to my sister and me to do something about it. We grabbed up some sacks, which were always kept handy for this use, and soaked them in the slough as we ran. The crop was not quite ripe and so was burning slowly, and we were able to put it out. But we discovered that the hems of our skirts were burned right off.

However, life by then was certainly more liveable, though never easy. And in spite of everything, my father's health greatly improved in the new adventure, and he was with us for ten more years, years that he really enjoyed, and for that, we were grateful.

Many Happy Incidences

Delia Bigelow Woolf describes her life as a child during the homestead-
ing era in the early 1900s.[1] From being kept warm by the stove to riding
horses, picking berries, and playing paper dolls with the Eaton's cata-
logue, Delia describes daily living in the Willow Creek district of Alberta.

I have always said that I've always been in a hurry. There seems to
be too much to be accomplished in this world. I came into the world
in a hurry—no hair, no fingernails, and weighing three pounds.
Dr. Harry Stackpool and my grandmother, Emily Bigelow, were the
first to welcome me. I have often heard my Grandmother Bigelow and
my mother tell how they took care of me for the first days, because
I was so small and it was necessary to keep me alive. Baby incuba-
tors were something long in the future. So I was kept in a shoebox,
wrapped in cotton and a baby blanket, or I suppose just a small piece
of cloth, and placed in the oven of a coal stove. I wonder what would
have happened had someone pushed the oven door shut! When I was
old enough and able to breathe properly, then Grandmother said that
I could come out of the oven.

I was real small, but the first horror of my life was when I became
panicky [when we crossed the Belly River by horse and wagon]. I can
remember screaming and screaming, and my mother trying to shut
me up, and I imagine she was filled with panic too, because she was a

non-swimmer. My father was a good swimmer and he thought nothing of it, but Mother must have been frightened almost to her death to cross that river. She crossed many rivers in her life, and streams that were swollen, because my father never was afraid. He just fastened the wagon box to the [wagon] and went across. In those days, there were many rivers that had to be crossed and many dangers that had to be feared. It wasn't until either a year or a year and a half later that a bridge was built over the Belly River.

We lived in the Willow Creek district. Our home was very picturesque. It was built down right near the river, and there were two forks of the stream. Between the two forks of the stream, the river and what we called the creek, was natural sand with trees, and that was our playhouse. We were never lonesome as children, because when there are nine children that grew to womanhood and manhood, there is always someone to play with.

There were many happy incidents in my childhood days. I can remember as a young girl when my uncle, William Bigelow, said to me one Christmas morning—Uncle Bill was always a great favourite of mine—"Santa Claus couldn't put your gift in your stocking, and you know what he did? He tied it in the barn." And it was a beautiful pony. I rode that pony and loved her until it was necessary to shoot her because she got fistulous withers.[2] And rather than see her suffer, she was shot. But to me, she was always something very precious. Father always saw that I had a good saddle. I had a beautiful lady's western saddle and good riding equipment.

In those days, you know, a horse was yours. If you had a good horse, you were quite proud. Each one of our family had their own horse, and there was always plenty of oats. We were told that each horse could have a tomato can of oats a day, but I'm sure they often had more than a tomato can, because we had to take good care of them.

I remember also as a child this favourite Uncle Bill was always giving me a nickel or a dime. My earliest recollection of food was that I loved beefsteak and I still do. At the time, I remember I was small enough that when one day he gave me a dime, I went down and threw it into the woodpile. We burned a lot of wood in those days, and the wood had to be cut. Anyways, I threw it in the woodpile and made a wish. It must have had some connection with wishing wells or something. When I came back and Uncle Bill said, "What did you do with your dime?" I said, "Well, I put it in the woodpile and made a wish that I could have beefsteak every day." And Uncle Bill said, "Oh, we have to go find it." But to this day, we never found that dime. After I understood that I had lost it, I looked and looked for it, realizing that it wouldn't bring me my beefsteak every day.

I remember as children we used to go berry picking. We always put up lots of berries—nature supplied them. In those days, fruit didn't come like it does now, so we went berry picking. It used to be sort of a picnic. We took our dinner and went across the river onto my father's ranch. There were acres of bushes where strawberries, serviceberries, gooseberries, and wild raspberries grew.

It was on one of these expeditions that a near-tragedy occurred. We always had horses that would run at the drop of a hat, as Father bred horses, and they were good horses. Wayne, my brother, took it upon himself to crawl up into the back of the buckboard buggy and, of course, frightened the horses, and they broke loose and ran. Father jumped on one of the saddle horses and took off after the runaways.

Horses, to me, have always had a kindred spirit with their owners and their riders. I can remember how, when he approached the buckboard, the little palomino mare, Flaxie, got close enough to the buckboard that her hair was scraped on her side so Father could reach the little boy out of the buckboard unharmed. Then he stopped the horses and, of course, they were tied again, and we were all lectured as to what we shouldn't do by getting into the buckboard or any place where the horses were when we were fooling around. Of course, Wayne was fooling around, getting out of work when he climbed up into the buckboard.

We had many, many happy experiences as a family. We used to go huckleberry picking, and of course we used to go to the mountains for that. If there was anyone who had to stay home, well, that was a sad day for the one that had to stay behind. There were times someone had to stay home when they weren't well enough to go for

▲ In this photograph, dated 1899, the children are hoeing the garden with their parents looking on. The family lived in the Huns Valley area of Manitoba. *Image NA-3080-3. Courtesy of Glenbow Archives, Archives and Special Collections, University of Calgary.*

some reason. It was quite a long trek to the mountains, and huckleberries were hard to pick. At times we stayed overnight, and then we came back.

We always had wild fruit pie for the twelve months of the year, because we picked the different berries. We picked them the years that we could. Naturally, there were some years that they were frozen, and then, of course, we had to have pies that were made from the milk and cream from the cows.

In those days, everything had to start from scratch. The eggs were gathered from the barn, and the flour milled at the mill. There was always someone that had a mill, and the farmers took their grist in to get their year's supply of flour. We didn't know anything about "two years' supply," but we always had nearly enough food to take care of us, and we bought the vegetables that would last in the cans. Carrots were raised in the garden, beets were raised in the garden, and all the garden produce was taken care of in a deep cellar, covered over for winter use. It was like going to the store once a week. You went down into the cellar if it was cold weather and brought the food up for a week. You would not open that cellar pit every day, because you would freeze what was in there.

We always milked enough cows on the farm, and there were always calves that were taken off the mother cow and raised on the bucket. Each of the boys had chores to do. One would have to feed the calves, one had to bring the wood in, one had to gather the eggs, and we all had things to do, even after we went to school. We didn't have time to get into trouble, because we had to hurry home from school to do what we had to do.

There was close companionship in those early days with the family and all the reading we did, and we were a family that liked to read—with kerosene lamps. Early settlers lived all their lives with a kerosene lamp, or maybe two or three that were taken from room to room. I sometimes marvel at the wonder that there weren't more of those lamps upset and more homes burned up, but the people were cautious and took care of what they had.

They took care of everything they had in those days, and it wasn't unusual for clothes to be handed down from the oldest child to the youngest child. Mother made most of our clothes. The little boys had their overalls purchased at the store, because they didn't make overalls in those days, but my dresses and my sister's dresses, they were almost, to a dress, made on the machine in the home.

There were dangers for children and dangers for older people. I can remember, when I was a very little girl, wandering into a wheat field, and I had on a sunbonnet. This was in the days when people could make the old slat sunbonnets, and my Grandmother Carlson had made me one. I always had a blue sunbonnet and my sister Gladys always had a pink one. Gladys was dark like my father, and I was light in complexion like my mother. Into the wheat field I went, and it was only the little breeze that stirred the wheat enough so that they could see my bonnet that saved me from being lost in the wheat field. What would have happened if they couldn't have found me? I know the first thing they would have thought was that I had drowned

⌃ A family going on a picnic in 1897. *Image NA-545-3. Courtesy of Glenbow Archives, Archives and Special Collections, University of Calgary.*

in the creek. While they were happy to find me, I got my lesson on not doing that again.

As soon as the catalogue came, when we were small children, we'd play paper dolls. We would go through the catalogue and pick out our paper dolls and, of course, it was months and months before we could cut them out. We made our own entertainment.

We didn't have family evenings or anything like that, because we did not know about them. But every so often, Mother and Father would sit us down, and they would say, "Now look, we want to know what you learned in school." Then we would have what we called recitation. I was quite quick at learning to quote verse, and I remember I learned at one time nearly all of *The Rime of the Ancient Mariner* [by Samuel Taylor Coleridge]. I learned many poems, and we would all tell what we learned about this or that.

We had a piano in our home, and my brother Reid learned to play quite proficiently—not professionally or anything like that, but he became quite proficient at the piano. We didn't sing. We weren't people that sang much.

We rode a lot, and we used to ride stake races, barrel races, and just in competition with our brothers and sisters and with our cousins and the neighbours. Later on, when the first 4H clubs were organized, I was too old, but the younger boys became members of the 4H clubs and they progressed along with it.

At school, I can remember I took part in the Christmas programs, the Easter programs, and most programs and the little plays that they presented. In the little country schools, they always had big Christmas programs, and every child was on the program. Santa Claus always came with gifts, and these gifts were always wrapped and handed to each child. It was quite a deal to get a Santa Claus that no one knew.

I always enjoyed picnics—school picnics, church picnics, family picnics. We had many family picnics. They were great for all the families getting together. In my father's family there were nine, and they all lived in the immediate area, and we could get together many times during the summer and during the winter. Winter were indoor parties and summer were outdoors. We all had large families, so there was always close association of cousins.

My father and mother died very young. I had only been married a little while when they both died within four years of each other. There is something that happens to a home when there is no place for children to go back to. I don't care who the family is. I have watched it all these years. After the mother and father go, there is no home, and people just don't go back if they have left the town of their birth. And it's rather tragic. As long as the parents stay alive, there is a goal to work towards, "We must go home to see our parents." But when that is gone, then there is no great reason for going home.

Adventure Is What I Wanted
and It Is What I Got

Joseph Hammerschmidt tells his tales of being a bachelor on the western prairies.[1] *Even though he applied for entry for a homestead, he did not have enough funds to make a go of it. He decided to work off-farm until he had enough money to invest in his property. In his memoir, Joseph describes working at different jobs and the adventures he experienced along the way.*

I want to relate my experiences. Let me make it clear at the very beginning that adventure is what I wanted and it is what I got. None of those hard-luck stories have any place in my narrative. I was young and full of pep. I travelled over the prairie sixty miles a day (not every day) on foot. I used to do the dogtrot.

I did not have money enough to start farming. So the best thing for me to do was to work for six months and then build a shack. I filed on my homestead unsight and unseen with an agent, William Bens, in Rosthern, Saskatchewan.

After working with a steel gang [maintaining the railway] for two months as a waterboy, I went with a grading outfit. At Lloydminster, we met the Barr colonists, who had come the year before. The boys [from the grading outfit] got drunk at Lloydminster. I was the only one that had a gun, but no ammunition or we would have shot up the town.

Whenever the boys got time, I would accompany them out into the country, looking for land. There was black soil, and grass knee-deep. I had my land or I would have taken some right there. One day at moving time, a wagon got stuck in a wet place. We hitched four horses on the buckeye.[2] As it jerked back, the front wheels jackknifed and the wagon tipped over. There was a great shout. Man under the load! We threw ploughs and scrapers in all directions and found the poor fellow with an upper broken arm. There was a doctor somewhere on the two-hundred-mile line, but where? East or west? The boss took the buckeye and went first west to the next outfit. There he found out that the doctor was east, so he took the injured man away with the buckeye the next morning. I learned later that one could alleviate the pain by putting hot and cold towels, dipped in hot and cold water, on the swollen part, changing them off continuously. If the swelling gets blue, apply the heat. This is well to remember. It may save a life or at least alleviate much pain. This is what is called the water treatment. It must be done at once, after the accident. Be sure to make it plenty hot!

There was one big thunderstorm that took all our tents down, except our sleeping tent, which we held down by sheer force. After two months with the grading outfit, it was time for me to go back to my homestead to build my sod house. Back to Battleford, two hundred miles away. I figured the best way would be to go on the Saskatchewan River that flows past the town. So I got my cheque, which I could only cash in Battleford. I travelled north to the river and made a raft, covered it with spruce boughs and set her adrift. I spread my blankets on top and went to sleep. When I woke up, I took my long pole to see how deep the water was and—umph! I was stuck on a sandbar. This happened several times during the night. Once I had to get out barefoot and lift and push with all my might to get the raft free again.

Next night, it started to rain. I found a nice spot at an overhanging bank. Levelling a place, I lined it with spruce boughs. I spread my blankets on it and went to sleep, often waking up. I heard foxes barking along the riverbanks, and the water babbling from the rain.

Pebbles would come loose from the overhanging bank. Showers of sand and gravel would rattle down. I was on the go before daybreak.

A large tree that I had seen the day before in the south, I could now see in the north. All this time I had only been making a long horse-shoe bend. It might take me another week to make Battleford, and my food supply was getting low. The north winds were also driving my raft back. I was making no headway. The water was low.

All at once, I came to a ferry. The tender told me that Lloydminster was about twenty-five miles away. I began to stretch my legs, and I got there before nightfall. I stayed overnight with some nice people. The lady of the house gave me a [drink] of milk. I soon found that there was no guile in those folks. They were honest and straightforward.

The steel had been making headway. In two days' walking, I got to the end of the steel. Then I hopped on board the work train to Battleford. It was the end of August. Nobody had heard a thing about Tramping Lake [where I wanted to go]. So, with a ham, a little flour, some ammunition, a pail for water, which I always kept filled, I started south towards Tramping Lake. Sixty miles of barren wasteland. Not a soul did I see anywhere. At last I came to Aroma Lake, west of what is now Landis. Here is where I saw a bunch of wild horses. They raised their heads high, dashed to and fro. Finally, they came very close to take a look at that strange intruder. Then they turned away and disappeared over the hills.

I saw some water. I hurried towards it. The weather was hot, I was sweating, the pack was weighing me down. The water in my pail was gone. I was famished. However, the water was salt and alkali. That would kill a person. O Lord, shall this be the end? I walked a hundred yards and there was a spring with cool, clear water. After ten more miles, I finally reached the settlement at Tramping Lake.

In conclusion, I would say I regret the passing of the old days. I used to travel a lot and enjoyed it very much.

In his memoir, Joseph also set out some hints for
surviving on the trail if a person became lost:

If you are lost in the woods, look at the trees. They are brighter on the southwest side, not on the south, since the sun is hottest in the afternoon. If you have nothing to eat, strip the bark off the tree. There is a thin layer under the main bark that a person can eat and live. If you travel over the prairie, the stones are bleached on the southwest and mossy on the north. If you have no food, there is a weed growing most places. Some of the stems got as thick as a little finger and have a bluish blossom. I used to keep my pockets full of those stems. They taste like rhubarb. Chew them as you go and swallow the juice. They quench the thirst and abolish hunger. If you have no matches, drive two sticks into the ground, gouge a hole on the top of both sticks and make a crosspiece pointed on each end. Put that in the holes, rub a belt of rope several times around the stick and rub back and forth. The friction will create a fire; however, you have to watch out as wool from your clothes catches fire easily.

A Little Girl's Thoughts

Phyllis (Kirk) Cardwell offers a new perspective about her home-steading experiences.[1] *Given that she was a child during that era, she recounts the stories that were important to her at the time. She comments on going to school, fighting a prairie fire, gardening, visiting neighbours, wearing second-hand clothes, and going to bed hungry.*

■

Here are a few of the experiences I have had with my parents on our homestead. Our homestead was halfway between Rama and Invermay, Saskatchewan, a mile from the railroad.

The name of our school was Mason School, and it was situated one mile and a half north of us. When I first started to attend this school, I took our dog, Jerry, with me. One morning when I got to school, I was just about ready to collapse. I can remember it all very well. I was just nine years old and I had to break my way through the deep snowdrifts. That morning it was sixty below, just as it was a few other mornings.

I don't think I will ever forget the day when a boy my own age came to see me. When I saw him coming, I ran into the bedroom and hid. I asked my mother to tell him I wasn't in, because I was so ashamed of the fact that I didn't have a pair of shoes to wear. Our folks had a hard enough time getting us shoes for the winter.

My parents and I moved to Manitoba when I was one and a half years old. We lived there until I was eight. In November 1910, we moved to Invermay and Dad filed on the homestead. We stayed in Invermay for the winter, until Dad put up a shack on the homestead for us. It sure was a hard winter. Dad was sick most of the time, but Mother saved the day for us little ones, as she was a dressmaker and I know she was a very good one. She once told us about a dress she made with one hundred and fifty pin tucks down the front and on the sleeves.

In April, Dad moved us out to the homestead where he had put up our shack. It was twelve by fourteen feet and was built of small, unpeeled logs. The roof was made of poles and slough hay, tarpaper, and sand earth. Our furniture was made of shiplap lumber. The doors and window frames were of the same material. We had a dirt floor for two or three years. We moved to our homestead with a team of oxen. I wasn't very old then, but I do not think I can remember a day more beautiful since.

We didn't have a cow then, so a kind neighbour let us have one of his for a while. The day he came to get it back, we had only a pail [of milk] left, and it was sour. One of my little brothers was crying so much that, finally, my mother could stand it no longer and gave him a drink. He downed it hungrily and then gave a startled cry, "Mother, that was sour."

There were fourteen children in our family. Eight boys and six girls. With no doctors or nurses, I had to be the nurse as I grew older.

One day early in the spring, a fire broke out from the railroad and came to our homestead. Dad had cut one hundred cords of wood that winter, and Mother and I had to save it as Dad was away working. I carried the water from the slough, and Mother put out the fire. It was an awful hard job. My feet were blistered.

The first garden we had was put in the ground that had been worked by pick and shovel as we had nothing else to work with. The earth was very rich and had two feet of black loam on it. We could grow celery thirty inches long in it.

There were a lot of early frosts, and if we didn't get up before sun-up and carry water from our well and water the garden, we wouldn't have one, and that was our living for the summer. I remember the frost coming out on the leaves after we had put the water on. It saved many a garden for us.

We had our garden fenced in from the chickens. One night, a fox got inside the fence, and the dog took after it. He could just keep up to the end of the fox's tail. At last, Dad got up and went out to the feed box where the food was kept for the stock. I had gone along with him to help him, so I got the lantern just in time to see a chicken go flying through the air. The fox was still in the barn, but the dog got him.

My brother Charlie was sick once with a cold, and Mother had a hard time trying to keep him in the house. A neighbour came to see us, and while he was there, he told Charlie that out there in the winter, it was very cold. If anyone died, they froze. Their feet would be sharpened and then they were driven into the ground. Mother had no trouble with Charlie after that.

We had a neighbour, Mrs. Lloyd. She was an elderly lady, but could make the most wonderful bread. I remember I used to beg to go and see her at least once a week. Mother couldn't understand why. Shameless to say, it was the big slices of fresh bread and jam she used to give me. We didn't have jam and I can still remember how good it tasted. One day, Mother let Charlie, Eva, and myself go to visit Mrs. Lloyd. At the time, Mr. Lloyd was burning brush, and the fire got away on him. Mother was so worried about us that she took the baby and had to leave the bread she was cooking after seeing the smoke in the distance. She had to go over the burned grass but wouldn't let us return that way. When we finally got home, the house was full of smoke and the cat had gotten into the tomato plants and tipped them all over.

One day Dad and I were raking hay with the team of oxen. Dad, at the time, was coiling. [To coil the hay, he used a pitchfork to gather the hay into a sloped pile that was about three feet high and four feet in diameter. This allowed the hay to dry, while at the same time it saved the hay from getting wet during a rainstorm, as the rain would run off the hay.] There was a slough nearby, and I noticed the team eyeing it very hungrily, so I got off and Dad started to rake. He got halfway around, and in went Dad, oxen, rake, and all. It was done so fast that he didn't have time to jump off. All we could see were three heads [sticking out of the slough].

Dad managed to buy a cow and a calf later on for twenty and a half dollars. But just like us humans, they got awful lonesome. So the only way Dad could keep her was to tie a log on her head with twenty feet of rope. One day she got away and took off into the water. I was told to go in after her. I did, but when I saw her in the water, I couldn't see as it was all moss on the bottom. There are two things I am afraid of, and that is water and being alone in the dark. So in went Dad. He went in and fell into a hole and went out of sight. When he got up again, he looked just like a big Christmas tree, all decorated and trimmed with brown moss. Mother was there, and I can still hear her laughing. She didn't laugh very often, as she had a hard life trying to feed and clothe such a large family.

My dad used to hand-tie the grain. The first few years we were on the farm, he cut it with a cradle and would take it to the nearest threshing machine. I'll never forget one day when they took a load of barley—I had been staying with my aunt the year before, and she had made a carrot pie which was very nice. I wanted Mother to make one, but she just couldn't figure out how to make a carrot pie, so she did not try it. So when they left with the barley, I thought this was my chance to make my pie. I had forgotten how Auntie had made it and I forgot the shortening. I just used salt, flour, and water. How I got the crust rolled out is a mystery to me. On top of that I just sliced the carrots like apples and put sugar and spice on it when I should have boiled and mashed the carrots and fixed them like a pumpkin pie. Carrot pie is very good when it is made right, and I hate to think of what Mother and Dad said when they saw my pie.

When I think back now, I often wonder how we lived. Mother had a lot of second-hand clothing given to her to make over for us. My sister Eve and I used to have our clothes laughed at at school, but Mother did her best to make them nice. I never had a new coat until I earned the money and bought it myself, and was I ever proud of it. Mother made old socks and even old coats into mitts for the boys, and I used to help her sew a lot. She could make suits, and she made Dad's shirts and pants. We sure had a wonderful mother.

I remember one Saturday night, we waited for Dad to come home from town. He had been away all week working, and he was to bring some flour as we did not have enough to do for the week. Dad did not come and we had to go to bed hungry, nothing in the house to eat. When he got home, Mother made pancakes for us kids and got us up to eat them. She felt so bad putting us to bed hungry.

The three of us older ones went to visit a neighbour one Sunday. While we were away, Mother was washing the dishes, and she put an empty syrup pail on the stove with a little water in it. She said she just set the lid on it, but the steam must have tightened it, because when she moved it to wash it, the lid flew up, and she got scalded with the hot water and steam in her face. One of the smaller boys ran to the barn to get Dad. All Mother had in the house was Vaseline, so that was what they used. When we got home, Mother was sitting by the stove with her winter coat on, and we couldn't see her eyes as her face was one big blister and she had the chills. I got her in bed with hot irons wrapped in a towel and tried to keep her warm. I looked after her, and I am proud to say she did not have a scar on her face when it healed up.

Christmas out there wasn't the same as it is now. We did not know about Santa Claus. I remember one Christmas, Mother made some candy and put some on a plate for each of us. We sure were happy kids to get that.

Eliza Jane (Brown) Wilson's Daily Journal

This selection of entries from Eliza Jane (Brown) Wilson's daily journal date from the late winter and spring of 1901,[1] when Eliza Jane resided with her husband and children on their ranch near Red Deer, Alberta. She was originally an immigrant from Scotland, while her husband was from England. He not only became a homesteader but was also a member of the North West Mounted Police. Her journal entries are intriguing, as they show what was of importance over the course of each day. She comments on the weather, discusses how the cattle and horses were faring, and expresses delight with visitors and with mail delivery.

■

FEBRUARY 26 There was frost this morning and it was very misty all morning. Could not see more than 50 yards away. The trees and everything was thickly covered with hoar frost. It cleared up to a nice day. It was thawing some. One of the milk cows fell in the stable this afternoon and broke her hind leg. We had to kill her. The bone was sticking through the flesh; her leg was just hanging by a bit of skin. Another cow calved. The calf is just about the size of a rat—made its appearance a month or two too soon.

FEBRUARY 27 There was frost this morning. It was a lovely chinook all day. The snow is almost gone. The water is standing in pools and running all over the prairie and in the creeks. I wonder how long it will last. We got mail today. I had a letter from Mrs. Wilson and a paper "The Sphere" with accounts and illustrations of the Queen's funeral. The calf died last night.

MARCH 1 No frost last night. It was not quite as mild as yesterday although it was thawing all the same. The creeks are still running with water. The upper dam burst this afternoon. March came in like a lamb, I wonder if it will go out like a lion. Busy writing an order to Eatons. Another cow calved too soon. Calf died, of course. What a beautiful moon-lit night, clear as day.

MARCH 2 What a terrible change in the weather today. It was 6 degrees below freezing and cold as there was a terrible strong wind sometimes. It got stormy several times and cleared up for a few hours and then came on a terrific storm which lasted for a few hours. We could hardly see the stable sometimes. It was drifting so much. It has been the worst blizzard we had had for years. The cattle were all covered with snow in a few minutes. Got mail today, only a letter and paper.

MARCH 11 Another change in the weather again. It was snowing during the night and early this morning. It cleared up and was a nice day, somewhat chilly but still it was thawing a little. The crocus heads are appearing and some grasshoppers are hopping about, also the gophers, but they have been out all winter. Another cow calved, that makes five now. Killed the poor piggie today. She was big and fat [for slaughter].

MARCH 13 Another nice warm day. Melting nearly all day. The snow is gradually disappearing. There is none left except what is in drifts. The water is standing in pools all round the buildings. The creek is still running. Branded the remainder of the calves which were too small to brand last year.

▲ A mare and her foal in 1890. *Image NA-2084-38. Courtesy of Glenbow Archives, Archives and Special Collections, University of Calgary.*

MARCH 14 Not much frost this morning. Nice day. Still keeps thawing. We can't have much bad weather now. Austine [a neighbour] passed this way to Queenstown [Alberta] with a load of coal, he was at Gleichen yesterday. "Sprite" foaled today, a little buckskin filly. "Pixie" is its name.

MARCH 18 Cows are calving nearly every day. Another cow lost her calf, came too soon.

MARCH 20 A lovely day so mild and warm. A great rush of water coming down the creek again. The prairie is almost dried up. It is nice to think spring is here at last. The air has such a refreshing smell. This winter has gone very quickly. I suppose it is all owing to Jack and Millie coming over so often [to visit]. There are quite a lot of little calves now. One cow calved last night—the calf was dead, a loss when a big one too. Another calved down by the lake; the boys are away for her.

MARCH 22 Nice day again. The wind was a little bit chilly for a while. It got much milder during the afternoon. The grass is growing green down at the lake. There was a large flock of geese that flew north today.

MARCH 23 The ice has gone out in some places and the river is unsafe to cross. George Walton [a neighbour] rode over this afternoon and he went through the ice.

APRIL 1 It was a very cold windy disagreeable day, got milder towards evening. There were big dark clouds but they passed away. The ground was white with frost this morning. It is very backward weather we are having for spring, and the cold is not yet out of the river nor is it melted in the dam.

APRIL 3 Winter is back again, snowing all day and very cold. It faired up towards the afternoon and the snow melted away pretty nearly again. It is very frosty tonight. I wonder if we will have good weather after this snow. We should have. We were having fine weather last spring at this time. My thin cow fell and broke both her neck and foreleg. It finished her all right. Only seven head now, and I will only have one calf this year. It's terrible! Terrible!

APRIL 4 There was frost this morning. It is terrible weather for this time of year. It was a nice day although the wind was cold, the sun was very nice and warm at times. There are one or two calves sick—none have died as yet. There was a very dubious looking one today. There were fifteen swan down at Snake Lake. Hope there is mail.

APRIL 12 It looked like winter again. Very cloudy and snowing slightly and cold a little. It cleared up and was a nice day though somewhat cloudy at times. It is a nice evening just now. All the ice melted in the dam a day or two ago. Some more calves are sick.

APRIL 13 Rather a cold morning and very cloudy and stormy-like. It passed over and was a nice day—a little bit cloudy and the wind coldish. There has been a crow flying around for the last few days. It is not often that we see these birds around here.

APRIL 26 It has been a very cold raw day, more like a day in the fall. It was very cloudy all day and stormy-like. I wonder when the real warm days will come. The river is quite low. Some more calves are sick again. "Maidie" died this morning. Such dreadful ill luck we have had with our horses! There is only one Clyde mare left now. It was pleurisy that ailed her. Our poor bunch has dwindled down, sadly.

APRIL 29 It was a beautiful day, the finest day we have had yet— almost up to summer heat. There was no frost at all. Lots of lightning in the evening. A large prairie fire started southeast from here.

APRIL 30 Rather windy day. Smokey a little. Jack [her husband] and a friend away out duck hunting. The men also tried planting potatoes. The two calves that were sick, died yesterday. Jack Marshall, Mr. Mitchell and Austine were down in the evening. We had a very nice little dance and had lots of fun.

MAY 7 Very cloudy and cool this morning, cleared up and was a nice sunshiny day. Jack left this morning. Will be back the first of June. Mr. Millie rode over this afternoon and brought some mail. The boys are hauling hay steady now.

MAY 8 Very cold all day and windy, feels as cold as a day in the fall. The weather is very unsettled, never two days alike. We are getting such quantities of milk and butter these days. And the cream is so rich and thick. The grass is long and thick and lovely and green. Mary [her daughter] has made two very pretty vases. They are really well done.

MAY 13 Very warm all day, almost a summer heat. Got a little bit windy towards the afternoon. Yesterday was a fearful hot day; the warmest we have had this spring. How beautiful the shrubbery is growing; one can almost see the leaves grow. Dave [her fifteen-year-old son] has gone for the mail, hope there may be a letter for me. Another dead calf today—was born dead.

MAY 15 Another fine day, very warm. There has been no frost at nights now for a few nights. This must be fine days set in at last. Vaccinated the remainder of the calves.

MAY 23 Raining all during the night and all day. It has been nice and mild all day, not cold a bit. Things will grow now after this, if it only comes heat. The mosquitoes will be fearful after this. A cow died this morning. The menkind killed her to put her out of her misery.

MAY 24 It has been a beautiful day, so mild and warm. The mosquitoes have been something fearful. They all disappeared by night. It got very much colder towards evening—quite chilly even. Some of the vegetables are up, very few though. We have quite a number of chickens out—twenty-six I think. We never had so many before, for such a long time.

MAY 28 Another very nice day. After dinner, Mr. Millie rode over and Jack [a friend] came about supper time. Poor chap, he is quite lame, hurt his kneecap.

MAY 29 Rather cloudy towards the afternoon and it was raining quite heavy for an hour or two in the evening. Brownie has lost her calf and Bill was away all evening hunting for it—couldn't be found. The wolfwillow is blooming and the whole air is perfumed.

JUNE 8 There was frost this morning. The potatoes and pumpkins are black. It is such a pity. There will not be many of the latter come, I'm afraid. There was quite a heavy shower of rain during the afternoon. The sun was very warm today but the wind felt chilly.

JUNE 12 What dreadful weather! Raining heavy the whole day. This is a rainy country, now it surely has been raining for nearly a fortnight. A week today!

JUNE 14 At last, it has stopped raining. Was a very nice day and warm, a little bit of wind started up and it was cloudy sometimes. Could not find the milk cows till half past four this afternoon.

JUNE 15 Cloudy and rainy at intervals. Seems as if it never were to clear up again. In the afternoon, Mr. Millie and George Walton rode over having a very nice time. As usual, brought the mail with them.

The Sod Shack

James Rugg details living in a sod shack on the prairie.[1] He also discusses the furniture that his family had in their home, the lack of sleeping space, the food that they ate, and the freezing temperatures in the house during the winter.

■

My grandson Jimmy has asked me to describe what it's like to live in a sod shack. The walls were built like laying bricks, the sods were cut about two feet long, were thirteen inches wide and four inches thick, with grass side down. We had one rough-made door about six feet high and two foot six inches wide, which was difficult to fit into the sod walls. The roof was a lean-to type, and there were three windows, two feet by twelve feet, with four lights in each, being set in two-foot-wide walls. Not much light could come in, and of course [there were] no storm windows. Many cold days in winter, an inch or more frost would gather on the inside of the windows.

To describe the house inside, it was twelve feet wide and twenty-two feet long; ten feet was curtained off for a bedroom, and the other twelve by twelve feet was used as a kitchen and living room. Later, a porch was added, which came in very handy. Poles with hay and sods on top were used for the roof over the bedroom. We used boards with tarpaper on top over the kitchen. The lumber for roof, door, and windows cost about twenty dollars.

One good fortune of having boards over the living room was the reasonable freedom from insects and dirt falling from the ceiling, but then the board roof had its faults, the result of my not fastening it down. The trouble happened when my father and I had gone to the bush twenty miles away for wood. A thunder- and windstorm came, and the board roof was lifted off and fell into a small garden alongside the house. On our arrival home in the afternoon, we found Mother unhurt in the kitchen without a roof over her head. You may be able to understand our dismay and Mother's terrible plight that afternoon.

I believe that I should relate briefly the circumstances on the arrival at the site of our first Canadian home. We had a meagre supply of tools, the main ones for building that we had to buy were an axe, bucksaw, claw hammer, and drawknife. Coming direct from London, England, we had none of the advantages of the homesteaders who had come from eastern Canada and the United States, many of whom brought horses, cows, etc., along with household furniture, dishes, and experience of the Canadian way of life. I should mention here that I had two years' experience on a farm in Killarney, Manitoba, before coming to the homestead here at Elstow, Saskatchewan, which helped in many ways, but much of the learning, being on a fairly well-established farm, wasn't applicable for us beginners on the prairies.

I mentioned earlier we had a dividing curtain between the bedroom and the kitchen and living room. Rough bedsteads were made of poles, the mattress cover being filled with hay, and the space under the beds being used for storing some of the boxes that were in the bedroom. My mother, father, and two sisters slept in this room. My brother and I had a movable, hay-filled mattress cover in the kitchen. To help the sleeping situation out somewhat, my elder sister and brother got work away from home for months at a time. The furniture, as far as I can remember, consisted of a nice mahogany table, two chairs to match, along with many boxes which came in handy for cupboards.

Father brought out twenty-two boxes, which contained our small amount of furniture, linens, blankets, dishes, tools, etc. I wonder now where we put everything. We bought a stove with oven, a sheet metal one which cost twenty dollars new. Of course, only wood was burnt then. We had a table lamp and barn lantern, along with candles. The stove was all the heating we had. In the winter, very many of the days and nights it froze in the house in spite of my getting up and putting wood in the stove many times during the night, the temperature often going to more than fifty below zero. There were no trees to protect us from the wind and snow. Again, owing to the fact of having nothing for plaster, the wind often blew through the cracks of the sod walls. Our wood was kept in a teepee, several loads in each piled in a manner to prevent the snow from piling over it. It also made shade from the wind when sawing it up with a bucksaw. I might add here that prairie fires, coming often, stopped any trees from growing in our district for over five years after we came to the homestead.

To continue, Mother found many dishes broken when opening the boxes. Our food for the first summer consisted mostly of wild rabbits (generally some of which were diseased, which had to be thrown away—this dulled our taste for rabbit), duck eggs, occasionally ducks, and salt pork, which we bought in large chunks. One thing we had was butter and milk from our cow. We sold butter to neighbours. I made a dash churn using a four-gallon stone crock, and the dash and top out of wood. It answered the purpose for years. Mother had brought a common square scrub board, and of course, all wringing was done by hand. We had a flatiron (handle attached), which was heated on the top of the stove. Mother made her own bread. A store at French, eighteen miles from home, supplied some of the necessary groceries. The post office was also located here. Later, the businesses at French were moved to Clavet when the railway was built.

Referring back to the groceries, I remember buying a twenty-pound box of dried apples, a fifty-pound bag of figs, three-pound cans of tea, and coffee at one dollar per can, sugar, oatmeal, syrup, flour. In fact, I spent fifty dollars I had earned driving oxen for a farmer for two months, who paid me with a cheque which I turned over to the storekeeper, who two weeks later sent me a letter saying that the cheque was no good. I wrote back to say that we hadn't any money and could only return most of the purchases. Shortly afterwards, he wrote saying the cheque had been accepted by the bank.

I forgot to mention our fresh pork. I had bought a Poland China sow from a Mr. Miller at French. They are, or were, a very fat type of pig, I believe raised extensively in the US at that time, 1905. Well, in July I had to bring this pig two miles on a very hot day, led by a cord tied to the hind foot. She was difficult to drive and near home she collapsed. Thinking she would die, I killed her, and we tried to cure some of the meat, but about three days later it spoiled. We hadn't money to buy fresh meat and no way of keeping it. I forgot we used to put some food in a pail and hang it partway down the well (that method of keeping food was used for some years). Late in the fall, we bought Ontario apples, mostly Spy, by the hundred-pound wooden barrel. In winter, our beef and pork were kept frozen outside the house and generally cut off in chunks with an axe or bucksaw.

I have endeavoured to give an idea of what it was like to live in a sod shack, which is only a small part of life of a family homesteading with practically no money in Saskatchewan, then the North-West Territories.

Freedom of the Wild

In this memoir, George Berkner recounts his life as a boy on his
family's homestead.[1] While he was herding cows one day, he not
only befriended a coyote, which kept him company, but he also
came to appreciate the wide open spaces of the prairie. He was also
fascinated by the wild birds who made the prairies their home.

◾

When I was a boy, we lived close to the railroad, there were no fences, and most of the country around us was unbroken prairie. Most of the homesteaders let their cattle roam and graze freely, rounding up the milk cows and bringing them home in the evening. Since we lived so close to the railroad, we had to continually watch our cows so they wouldn't get on the track and get hit by a train. Herding those cows was my job, so every day I would take a stick and sit on a hill where I wouldn't lose sight of them. Sometimes they would take a notion to head for the track, and that is when my troubles started, for once range cattle decide to go in a certain direction, it is pretty hard to make them change their minds.

When I first saw my coyote friend, I was sitting on a little knoll one morning, amusing myself weaving chains out of slough grass. I looked up and saw him sitting near some wolf willows, watching me, and we sat there watching each other for a while until I finally decided to chase him. I got up, grabbed my stick, and started towards him. He just got up and looked at me, as much as to say, "Well, what do you think you are going to do?" As I came closer, he trotted off, looking over his shoulder, and made for those willows. I finally went back and sat down on my mound. I looked up and, sure enough, there he was again, a little closer this time. He was standing there looking at me, as much as to say, "Well, come on, boy, aren't you coming?" When he saw that I wasn't coming after him, he started to sniff at a dirt mound nearby, then started to dig, and in no time had dug out a bit fat mole. He played with it for a while, throwing it up in the air and catching it in his mouth, then gulped it down, and trotted off down the hill.

By now our cows had wandered off out of sight, so I took my stick and went looking for them. I found them drinking at a slough nearly half a mile away, so I sat down close by where I found some snake-grass to chew. Snakegrass is sweet to chew and very good to quench your thirst. I looked up and there was that pesky coyote again, watching me from the top of a hill. I crouched down in some tall grass and waited to see what he would do. He just sat there for a while, then trotted off down the hill into some bushes. I couldn't see him now, but I knew he was sitting in that bush, watching me and waiting to see what I was going to do next. I sat there a long time, until I got tired and got up. Well, hello, there he was right behind me, not thirty feet away. I made for him, brandishing my stick, but he just trotted ahead of me, looking back with a mischievous look on his face, as if to say, "Well, come on, fellow. Give me a good chase. This is fun!"

I herded those cows all that summer, until my dad got our pasture land fenced, and every day my coyote friend would show up to play our little game of hide-and-seek until he would get tired of playing hard to get and finally go off hunting somewhere. Then one day he did not show up. After a few days went by with no sign of him, I began to get worried and used to go roaming around the hills and hollows looking for him.

By now, the pasture fence was finished, so I didn't have to herd the cows anymore, but I still roamed the prairies, not just in search of my coyote, but because I loved the freedom of the wild. The country at that time was a small boy's paradise, dotted with wildflowers of every colour. There were some big sloughs that never dried up, teeming with thousands of ducks and wading birds. Most of these small lakes were surrounded with tall reeds and bulrushes, which supported scores of muskrat families, both for food and material to build their houses.

Besides the life in and around our sloughs and ponds, our prairie was the home of many four-footed critters ranging in size from the little field mouse to the mule deer. Of course, the day of the buffalo was long gone, but the hills were still strewn with their bleached bones, in mute testimony of the way they had been unmercifully slaughtered in the past. When my father told me they were buffalo bones, I used to ask him, "Why did they kill them all? Were they that bad?" I was still too young to figure out why people would kill off a certain animal until all one could find was their bones scattered all over the country.

I knew the prairie country around our homestead like the back of my hand for miles in every direction. Since there was still no school in our district at that time, and no children to play with, I roamed around to my heart's content. I got to know the habits of the animals. I knew where all the different birds nested and how they got their food. I would sit and watch a big hawk circle high in the sky, then come plummeting straight down and catch a gopher in his talons and carry him off to the nest in a big old poplar tree. I knew that the mallard duck nearly always nested on high ground, well away from water, so the skunks wouldn't find her eggs. There was the redheaded woodpecker that had bored a hole in a telegraph pole by the railroad for her nest. I lay hidden in the grass and watched big flocks of prairie chicken going through their dance rituals in the morning sun. The deer got so used to seeing me that they no longer bounded off when they saw me. They would just stand and look at me for a minute, then go right on feeding.

Those were the days when you could go out in the morning and hear meadowlarks and smaller songbirds singing their hearts out. There were always flocks of ducks flying back and forth from one slough to another; the wading birds, such as snipes, plovers, and sandpipers, were always busy looking for their particular kind of food. In the spring, great flocks of Canada geese would settle down on some of the larger sloughs to rest a while and feed on wild rice before going on to their nesting grounds up north.

▼ Many people enjoyed their leisure time exploring the prairies and appreciating its natural beauty. This photograph shows a young woman enjoying a day's outing with her dog (a companion who was taking the photograph), and two saddle horses. *Image NA-1549-2. Courtesy of Glenbow Archives, Archives and Special Collections, University of Calgary.*

Things changed gradually as the country became more settled, and more and more land was broken up until, finally, there was very little virgin prairie left. Soon the sloughs started to dry up, so the waterfowl had to go farther and farther north to find feeding and nesting grounds. The ducks and wading birds were not the only ones that were having a hard time, for as the prairies diminished, some birds, such as prairie chickens and pheasants, sought sheltered spots in farmer's fields to build their nests, only to have their eggs destroyed when seeding started.

Not only was the farmer's plough giving our game birds a bad time, but as our town grew into a city, every fall hordes of hunters would invade our land—their sole ambition seemed to be to see how many birds they could bag before the season closed. They also left many wounded birds to die in agony or become prey to predators such as coyotes, badgers, and weasels.

In the homestead days, our country roads were nothing more than wagon trails, and there was still enough natural prairie left along our roadways for some of our ground-nesting songbirds, such as the meadowlark and song sparrow, to find places to lay and hatch their eggs. But as time went on and cars became more plentiful, the municipalities were forced to build roads suitable for that mode of travel, so the last bit of prairie ground went before the grader blade.

The beginning of this story dates back seventy years, and as I sit now and reminisce, I am thankful that, as a small boy, I had the opportunity to see this land and all its wild creatures before man drove many species out of existence forever.

Appreciation for Her Mother

In this memoir, Olive Lockhart describes her life as a young girl living with her family on the homestead.[1] She discusses many of the chores that she had to help with, how difficult life was for her parents, and the hard work that was involved with every task. She also highlights the food that was gathered and prepared for the daily meal.

■

At home, that first year or so, my brother and I led a very free and happy life. We helped with little chores of course—wood, water, gardening—but there was no compulsion about it most of the time. We had a few hens, which were cooped up in a tiny cage close to the house. They had the scraps from the table, but we were all hearty eaters so not much was left, and there were always cats and a dog to feed. We pulled weeds and wild grasses with seeds on them, and dropped then into the chickens' small run, but they gradually died. We did not understand that the poor things needed grain. Had they been let out, they could have found plenty of food, insects, grasshoppers, etc., but we were totally ignorant of how to run a farm.

It must have been terrible for my poor mother. She had lived in a city most of her life with all the then-known conveniences—running water, gas lighting, and indoor plumbing. Here, water had to be dipped out of a slough and heated on the wood-burning stove before doing the washing. Clothes were rubbed on a plain piece of board (not even a glass washboard at that time) in a galvanized iron washtub. It was back-breaking work, as were all the jobs on the homestead. There was a shallow well for drinking water, about eight feet deep. One spring, the water tasted queer, so Father emptied the well and found twenty-seven rabbits at the bottom of it. It is a wonder we were not all sick. Often, mice and frogs would get in there and die; then the job of dipping out the water would have to be undertaken again.

Father bought his first cow from his brother, Sam, for thirty dollars. She had a calf with her and was a fairly good milker, but was afraid of any person but Father, so he always milked her. We kept well away, as at the least sign of someone else she would kick out and spill all the milk in the pail, two gallons or more. She gave Father twelve calves in as many years, ending up with twin male calves, which we named Max and Maxim. In the meantime, we had acquired other cows by raising or buying them.

Our first cream separator was not much larger than a coffee grinder. Father made a wooden bench for it with a seat for the operator to sit on. It was a VERY slow job, but easy to turn so that we children could do the job. Later on, when we had much more milk, a larger machine was purchased, and the men put up a small shed made with rough poplar lumber, which we grandiosely called "the dairy." This was my particular domain. After the men had run the milk through, with my help in changing pails and refilling the tank as needed, I had the pails and separator to wash and scald twice a day—then churned the cream into butter, and made the butter into pound prints.

I was a dreamy, imaginative child and spent many hours alone among the trees with imaginary companions, also wandering about seeking wild fruit, which was far from abundant on our farm. I think the soil was poor. Some people had raspberries and strawberries in abundance. The latter had a very fine flavour but were tiny. I could spend a whole morning and come home with no more than a cupful. Some years were better than others. There had been a bush fire, and the next year the canes would spring up and bear abundantly. There were a very few gooseberries too, and one tiny pot of jam was very precious to Mother.

How she managed to keep us all fed and clean was a miracle. Of course, we had a big garden each year. I had a little patch of my own, and one year I grew a lot of citrons. They were round and green with pretty white markings, and made splendid preserves with lots of sugar and lemon, or ginger flavouring. Father took half a dozen of them to Invermay to try and sell them for me. No one wanted them, and he had to practically beg the people at the hotel to give him fifty cents for the lot, as he told them "my little girl will be so disappointed." It was like this with almost anything we grew or raised. Most people had their own gardens, and no one had money to buy from others. Sometimes Father was able to sell a load of firewood in the town.

In reading over my father's autobiography, I saw the following, and it is typical of prices at that time.

> In 1907, I bought three sows and a boar, all young, and paid seven cents a pound, live-weight. Although they had fairly good litters, the price dropped and I remember taking seventeen pigs, three months old to Sheho. All I could get for them was two dollars each. They had cost me far more than that to raise. However, I could not take them home again as there was no feed for them. There was no better success with the rest. I sold a sow and six pigs for twenty-five dollars, and those I butchered brought only five cents a pound. That same year, I worked on the railroad. Had to rise at 4 a.m., feed pigs, get my own breakfast and walk three miles to the starting point. After shovelling gravel all day, arrived home 7 p.m., again fed pigs and self, and crawled into bed. No doubt I lost at least one hundred dollars on pigs that first year. For one thing, I had to buy feed instead of growing it, and sometimes could not even buy it. But later on, I had my own flour, bran, and shorts, and wheat grits (cream of wheat) by taking wheat to the mill in Sheho, thus laying in a year's supply. Also, I never again bought more than two young pigs at a time, one to breed and one to fatten and butcher for the household.

Most of the time seemed to be spent plucking wild ducks and cleaning them ready for cooking. The sloughs were all overflowing with water as it was at the peak of a wet cycle. In the middle of some sloughs were the remains of fences where early ranchers had built and fenced haystacks during the former dry cycle, which proved the theory of seven years of drought and seven years of heavy rain. The sloughs were teeming with wildfowl at the time, and they were the main source of our food supply. We also used some of their eggs, when still fresh, taking just one or two from a nest so that the duck would not desert the rest.

In the wintertime, it was rabbits, which abounded in the thousands. On moonlight nights, to go out and see them hopping around among the frost- and snow-covered trees made one feel they were in fairyland! The skinning and preparing of them was not too pleasant, but they made good eating. However, we all grew heartily sick of them, and most people have not wanted to touch rabbit meat since then.

Of course, we raised chickens and had plenty of eggs, each cooked in every known way to provide variety. Our big garden gave us plenty of vegetables. Until they were ready, I gathered large pans full of pigweed (wild spinach) and dandelion greens. At times there would be a plentiful supply of mushrooms. Whatever we could find that was at all edible, we used.

In the fall, the root vegetables from the garden were stored in the cellar, which was just a little hole under the house, with a flap that lifted up into the living room. Almost every year the potatoes froze down there in the coldest weather, and the smell of boiling potatoes after they have been touched with frost is something I, for one, never forgot. Even if we could not eat them, they had to be boiled for the pigs and chickens. Turnips do no hurt to be touched with frost, but most other vegetables are ruined. Then, when the spring thaw occurred, this little cellar hole filled with water right up to the floorboards, so everything had to be cleared out before that. The house was built on a low-lying land with sloughs on every side.

All of this was a lot of work every day, Sundays and holidays included. Cows cannot be neglected because it is Sunday. Calves, pigs, and chickens must all be fed and cared for. Only those who have lived on a farm can have any idea of the hard work it entails, the long hours of labour both summer and winter.

Grace to the Haggis

John Allan recalls events that occurred while he lived in a
"Scotch settlement" near Battleford.[1] In one story he describes
the effects of whisky drinking on those attending a haggis cere-
mony, while his other stories focus on raising pigs. Grace to the
Haggis refers to the Selkirk Grace, a prayer that is spoken before
the haggis is eaten. The grace is attributed to Robert Burns.

They used to call our settlement the Scotch settlement at first, as there was so many of us from Scotland. We brought our bibles and Robbie Burns poems with us and had religious services and Burns celebrations. We formed a literary and debating society and had lectures and entertainment which were both humorous and entertaining.

At our Burns celebrations, we had the haggis piped in in real style, and a banquet with toasts to the King. To the land of our birth. To the land of our adoption. To the banner province of Saskatchewan. And, of course, to the ladies. We drank the toasts in lemonade. No liquor allowed, but on one occasion a bootlegger arrived on the premises. I was giving the address to the Immortal Memory, and I noticed that some of the men were going outside. After a while they would come in, seemingly very pleased with themselves. Then others would go out and come back equally happy.

▲ Two fellows enjoying a drink in 1896. Note the Scottish attire worn by the person on the right. *Image PA-4043-2-13. Courtesy of Glenbow Archives, Archives and Special Collections, University of Calgary.*

I told a joke about the Duke of Argyll, and then one of the men who had gone out too often and was standing in the lobby, leaning against the side of the door, commenced saying he was a better man than the Duke of Argyll and kept repeating it till some of them took him to a caboose outside, where he fell asleep. I heard that the old gentleman who was to give the Grace to the Haggis also went out and was offered a drink, but he said, "Na, I wonna tak a drink the nog for I hae tae gae the Grace to the Haggis," and added that "the women in there hae noses like greyhounds an they wad smell

Sandra Rollings-Magnusson

the whisky." But he bought a bottle and hid it somewhere in the schoolyard, saying he "wad hae a good dram" later. While he gave the Grace to the Haggis, some of them who saw him hide his bottle, stole it. My poor father lamented because he had not taken his dram while he got the chance.

The snow was very deep, and most of us had to travel by sleigh when going home. The man who thought he was as good a man as the Duke of Argyll was standing at the back of the sleigh, and when the horses started up he fell over the back of the sleigh. His hat fell off but he had a bottle of whisky in each hand and kept a firm grip on the bottles. The driver was unaware that our friend had fallen out till I told him that the Duke of Argyll had fallen overboard. Afterwards, he was known as the Duke of Argyll locally.

On one of these occasions, I was sitting next to a native of Russia, and when a lady dropped a spoonful of haggis on his plate, he seemed surprised and asked what he should do with it. I told him to eat it and he slowly rolled the haggis around his plate and commenced to eat it. He wasn't making good time, so I told him to put it in his pocket and eat it when he got home, which he did.

The ladies used to grind the rolled oats for making the haggis in a little coffee mill which a man had brought out from Ireland. We always had plenty of rolled oats, as one of our number bought half a ton of rolled oats in Battleford.

As for another homesteading story, we had quite a job keeping hold of the first pigs we bought. One little pig got its head in a syrup pail. The handle of the pail went behind its ears and it could not get it off. It took two days before we could catch that pig. Whenever we got near her, she would shake the pail on her head and bound off again.

One of our neighbours, who was having trouble with a big sow, was taking no chances when her husband went away to the bush for wood. She got hold of the old sow, and setting it up on its hind end against the clothes pole, she bound the clothesline around the pig and the clothes pole. When her husband and myself came home from the bush and saw the pig fastened to the clothes pole, her husband turned to me and asked if I had ever seen a sight like that before. To which I replied, "No." He then said, "That's what you get for bringing city-bred women to the prairies."

Before finishing with pigs, one of our neighbours built a place of sods shaped like a beehive, with a hole at the top to feed the pig through. He was proud of his handywork and asked me to see how the pig was thriving. When I looked inside, I could see no pig, only a well-used utensil which had been used to feed the pig with. That pig was never found.

A Dirty Deal

In this memoir, Gordon Wolseley Stewart expresses his frustration (and his fellow farmers' frustration) with the grain elevator companies and the CPR when dealing with harvested grain.[1] Using a number of examples, Gordon outlines the unfairness of the situation and discusses how the farmers banded together and formed a co-operative movement.

While working for a living and to gain experience in farming, I was just a hired man and was not brought into any conversations among people I was with. But I did realize that there was a considerable discontent among the farmers over the way they had to sell their grain. The elevator operators had the say as to what grade the wheat was that was brought to the elevator. The farmer could either take what the operator offered or go to another elevator, in which he would get the same treatment. The operator decided what grade the wheat was and what amount of dockage [would be deducted for] each load.[2] When I was hauling grain for the farmer I was working for, I was astounded at the treatment the farmers got, the grades given for their wheat, and the amount of dockage taken off each load, and I was then just a kid with no experience along those matters. Later, when I got my own grain to sell, I knew what a fight the farmers were really having.

About that time, some farmers took the bull by the horns, as it were. I think of men I did not know but whose names were very much

⌃ A grain elevator in 1905, with the railway station in the distance. *Image PA-1889-101. Courtesy of Glenbow Archives, Archives and Special Collections, University of Calgary.*

a topic of conversation. I think of the Partridge brothers of Sintaluta, John Millar of Indian Head, and Bill Motherwell of Abernethy (the latter later became minister of agriculture in the King administration at Ottawa). These men had a meeting with officials of the CPR and the Department of Agriculture. Out of that meeting there came the ruling that when a farmer wanted to ship his own grain, he could have that privilege. Up to that time, he couldn't ship a bushel except through the elevators, taking the grade and dockage of the elevator company. The new ruling was called the "car order book," referring to a book kept by the railway agent. Each farmer could sign for a car, if and when available. That was a step in the right direction, but far from perfect.

The elevator companies signed the book as well as did the farmer. The name at the top of the list got the car spotted [left on the track] where he designated. The car had to be loaded within twenty-four hours or demurrage was charged against the car. Many farmers could not get equipment enough to get a carload of grain into the car in a reasonable time, so lost the car. It was not really a bad rule, for otherwise a car could be held up for too long a time while a farmer who lived some distance from the loading platform was hauling his grain to the car. For that reason, many farmers built portable granaries and placed them in the town and hauled the grain to their granaries. They could then load their car in a day.

But the railway and elevator companies got around that. For instance, when the harvest was over and I was waiting for a chance to go back to the homestead, one of the elevator men asked me if I wanted a job to work all night. I sure did, and he said to come around at 9:30 PM that night and he would give me a job levelling grain cars. He would pay me a dollar for the night's work (which I never did get). At 5:30 PM, a train of empty boxcars came to town and was spotted at the elevators, two or three to each elevator depending on the capacity of the elevator. It was a Saturday and raining. What farmers had been in town had gone home by that time, and there were no telephones or cars or any way farmers could be notified that a car had come. The rule was that when cars came to the point, a list was made of the men eligible for a car, as per the car order book. If the car was not claimed within two hours, that list was taken down and a new list of the next eligible on the car order book was posted up. In two hours, if the car or cars were not claimed, that list was taken down and the cars were given to the elevators.

When I went to the job at 9:30 and found out what had happened, I thought what a dirty deal the farmers on the car order book got that evening. True, on Monday morning there was room in the elevators for a lot of grain, but it meant those who hauled their own grain had to take it to the elevator and take their grade and dockage.

That and other things, somewhat along the same lines, were the reason the farmers got together and formed the Saskatchewan Co-Operative Elevator Company, which was very successful and the forerunner of the Saskatchewan Wheat Pool. The Co-Op gave the farmer what was coming to him from his sale of grain.

Spring 1903 was very late in coming, and the question was what to plant for crops. Flax was one possibility, and several settlers (they were coming in quite fast to the district) said that they were going to sow some. Well, the ones who were going to plant flax were almost all Americans who had some experience with the grain, but a silly idea got around that flax, or a couple of crops of it, would ruin the land. A lot of the Canadian settlers, myself among them, had had no experience with flax and did not use it except on a few acres as an experiment. That experiment showed that flax was indeed the thing to grow on that land, for wheat was not as reliable then as it became in later years. I got a few welcome dollars from the flax and almost nothing from the wheat that season. I had as heavy a crop of wheat as I ever had, and it did look so good, but it did not ripen. An early frost and a heavy scourge of rust finished off what had promised to be a bumper crop. It ended up as a few bushels of No. 2 wheat, worth very little at the elevator. Still, we did get money, which was better than the nothing we had been getting the past years.

Another season I put in about eighty acres of flax. Half of the field was the nicest crop I had ever seen, but the other half did not look so good. I had so many nice things said about the good part, until it was threshed and the good-looking part of the field yielded almost nothing. So little that we were very depressed again, falling, as it were, from wealth to nothing—in dreams, that is. I remember the discussion around the dinner table that day as to what had happened to that crop. The man who owned the thresher was disappointed too, as he was doing the job at so much a bushel. But when the poor-looking half was threshed, it almost filled the granary! How it ever yielded as it did is still a mystery.

Then came the hauling of the grain to get some money out of it. I was able to buy a wagon and grain box, payable when I got the grain out, with interest of 8 percent before due and 10 percent after due till paid. Well, I had to have it, and as it happened, when I got the returns from the grain, I had no trouble paying. What I had not figured on was that I would have to pay such a toll in selling the grain.

The first load was flax, and there was only one elevator in the town that was taking flax. When I had loaded it, a little was spilled, and I took great pains to gather up the spilled grain and put it in the wagon box. But in cleaning up, I must have got a wee lump of dried mud, so when the elevator man got a sample from the load, he got the lump and put it in the screen. The test showed 12 percent dockage, and I refused to accept the settlement with that amount of dockage, as there was not a weed seed in the whole load. While I was objecting to the settlement, the operator had elevated the flax and mixed it with other flax that was very dirty, so I had no recourse but to take the cheque. That taught me a lesson, and I was not going to be caught in that predicament again. I bought lumber and made a portable granary that I could haul home, and I brought the rest of the flax from the farm and stored it in the new granary until such time as I had it all in, and maybe I could get a small boxcar or make a deal with an elevator before I hauled him the balance of the crop. It didn't work that way.

Due to my inexperience with handling flax, I did not know that special bracing was needed in a granary—the one on the farm had been fine. With another hundred bushels to bring in, the granary burst, and what a mess. I did not get any sympathy from the elevator operators, one of whom said he would take it in as he had another customer who had some to get rid of. So I had to haul the crop of flax to the elevator anyway, and had the work of building and moving that granary back to the farm—a distance of twelve miles. I was learning, but always the hard way. The rest of the flax did not have a 12 percent dockage, though, which was something.

I had some wheat to dispose of that fall too, and I took a load to the elevator. "My, but that looks like nice grain," the elevator operator said, "but I can only give you No. 3 for it. See those big kernels?" I did, but could see no difference except in size from the others. He said, "The millers don't want those in the wheat, they don't make good flour," or some such excuse. The other elevator I went to had the same yarn, so I had to let the lovely wheat go for a No. 3 and dockage on top of that.

In cleaning the wheat for seed, I ran it through the fanning mill fast so as to get the best, and ran over the sieves any shrunken or off-size kernels. That meant I had a lot of grain that had a lot of chaff and other things that were screened out. There was a change of operators at the elevator that I had taken the grain to the fall before. I went to the new man and told him what I had done, and he said to bring it to him, he would see what he could do with it. He put it through the sampling screen and said it was nice wheat and he would give me No. 1 for it—less, of course, the dockage.

From what I had seen as a hired man hauling grain for farmers, and what personal experiences I had, I understood why men were properly fed up with the elevator companies and the CPR. They seemed to work hand-in-hand to beat the producer. That kind of treatment was what brought on the organization of the Co-Operative Elevator Company, and later the Wheat Pool.

Sometime after the above experience took place, I was sitting in an elevator engine room, where the power to operate the machinery was generated, and got into discussion with a man who was a stranger in the district. The conversation turned to the difference in the method of handling the grain from past years, when all grain was hauled in two-bushel sacks. He told me it was easier then to swipe a few bushels from the farmers than it was at the time we were talking. He told me he was a grain buyer in past times, and when the farmer handed the sacks of wheat to the operator to empty into the scale hopper to be weighed, the operator kept a hole in the floor opened. He would throw the odd empty sack down the hole. Then, when the load was all in the hopper, the man on the load [the operator] would object to the weight, so the number of sacks was counted and multiplied by two bushels. Maybe you lost a sack or two on the way to town, which, unfortunately, was the case in many trips, so the operator had no trouble with the driver over a couple of lost bushels. Just count the empty sacks.

Here is an example of what went on at the grain elevator. One of the operators where I used to haul my grain would hire a man to run his farm while he would run the elevator. This farmhand was a brother-in-law of my best friend in those days. In one of our discussions, he told me that he usually shipped a car of wheat in his name for the operator, which the operator had collected from overages. From my experiences, I believe he told us the truth. The operator could not ship in his own name.

Here is another experience the farms at Bechard, Saskatchewan, had some sixty-or-so years later that shows the one-sided neutrality of the railroads. I was a member of the local wheat board committee and was asked to see the railway superintendent at Regina on the matter of getting boxcars to unload some of the grain in the Wheat Pool elevator at that point. After some niceties, he asked what my trouble was, and I told him that I had been asked to see if some cars could be sent to our shipping point so the growers there could get the grain out, using our own facilities. He had some papers on his desk, and after looking at them he said the Pool elevator there was the only one filled, and the others had lots of space. Until all the elevators were filled, they could not put cars into Bechard. Shades of 1904! I could not see much difference between taking cars from the farmers who were under the car order book and flatly refusing cars until the opposition elevators were filled to capacity.

I have been asked several times if I ever saw a satisfied farmer. I have to ask who would be satisfied under like conditions?

The People of Regina

Mrs. W.T. Billing came to Regina, Saskatchewan, from London, Eng-land, in 1912, as a young single woman who was looking to be employed as a schoolteacher. Once in the city, she could not find work immedi-ately, so instead she spent time writing down her thoughts comparing life in western Canada to life in London.[1] Her descriptions of early Regina are fascinating, as she not only describes its ongoing develop-ment (particularly its redevelopment after the 1912 cyclone), but also discusses the attitude and character of the people who lived there.

The year was 1912. I had travelled to Montreal from England on my way to take a post as a teacher in Saskatchewan. The journey from there to Regina was not pleasant. In London, at the Canadian offices, I had been told that Saskatchewan was short of teachers and would welcome any English college-trained teacher with a first-class certifi-cate. Once in Regina, I bought a teacher's magazine and newspaper. There were no advertisements for teachers in Saskatchewan. What to do now?

For a day or two I wandered the wooden sidewalks of Regina. The following descriptions are extracts from letters I wrote at that time:

Regina is a nice little place, but the ruins are appalling. [A cyclone had devastated the town a short time previously.] They are build-ing it up again as quickly as possible, but the havoc wrought by the

➤ Some single women sought paid positions. Being a teacher offered independence, prestige, and social status. However, once they married, social convention dictated that they would quit their jobs to take up the more important work of being a wife and mother. *Sandra Rollings-Magnusson Collection.*

cyclone must have been terrible. Mrs. Songhurst [the owner of the rooming house where I was staying] says houses were carried intact 100 yards and planted. Many people received terrible injuries, in fact not enough escaped to tend the injured. She says hundreds lost everything they possessed, every stick of property, but they went about with white faces helping others. Of all of the churches, the only ones left standing were the Anglican and Roman Catholic. The latter was damaged but the former not at all—a great portent, says my landlady, a keen Anglican. Last night we had a storm such as is common here, but I could not have imagined. The lightning flashed up the garden path, along the grass, everywhere, but only one peal of thunder to twenty to thirty flashes. Then the wind rose with a funny whirring noise and then all the boards creaked as though hundreds of windows were cracking. Then the hail came down. I have never imagined anything like the sound of it. It was as though every building in the city was crashing down and yet it did no damage. It was soon over. It was the first storm since the cyclone and was not considered bad.

Mrs. Songhurst says that one day she was walking in the street when the lightning lifted her from her feet and wrapped around her three times, yet did not hurt her. With all the storms, she never remembers any damage done by lightning. I'm afraid this is a rather frightening picture of Regina, but it is not often like that. The weather is very hot now, and yet one does not feel at all drowsy and can work and walk easily—I know I should be downright miserable in this heat in England, but I do not mind it here. The winters are fearful according to accounts. It is quite common to have one's eyelashes frozen so that one cannot open one's eyes and yet everyone seems to have enjoyed them. They tell me terrible tales about the weather in winter, until I nearly die of horror, and yet today is what we should call hot in England, but here everyone is saying it is cold and wearing thick costumes. I have been looking at the heating

apparatus this morning. Mrs. Songhurst says the houses are beautifully warm in winter. Some people wear cotton frocks indoors but not out.

The atmosphere of the place is quiet briskness. There is no worry or scurry as in England. The people do not wear that worried, nervy look, but are smart and cheerful looking. Everyone dresses very neatly though clothes are extremely dear. I have seen no one with clothes approaching shabbiness. Everyone thinks they work hard, but they do no such thing. I hear a good deal through the people coming in and out of Mrs. Songhurst's house. They are not lazy, for when the work is in front of them, they do it with a will, but if they feel like a walk or a chat, they think nothing of leaving what they are doing, no matter what subordinate position they hold, and going for a walk or taking an hour off. It is a land of splendid opportunities, but it is a young man's land. There is plenty of work. Anyone knowing shorthand and typewriting could get a post any day at fifty dollars a month at least. Anyone knowing, in addition, bookkeeping and a little French or German can earn extraordinary amounts. Those who get richest quick are builders, carpenters, and engineers. Carr, a young carpenter, is making piles of money and has the real estate fever. Living is shockingly dear. I paid twenty-five cents (about a shilling) for a pair of wooden knitting needles and they were off, but they were the nearest to a pair they had.

Mrs. Songhurst says poultry farming, which my parents wished to do, is not profitable here because the fowl die in winter. Eggs are thirty cents a dozen in the summer. Fowl for the table cost about a dollar each. Jam and marmalade are quite unknown because fruit is terribly expensive. Plums are about three cents a pound but peaches only two cents each and apples about the same and so are oranges. We get scarcely any vegetables and no fresh fish. To show the cost of living here, the smallest coin is five cents, and you can buy nothing for that except stamps and newspapers. There was a little ten-cent store. One went down a few steps into a dark little room where everything was priced at ten cents. No one thinks of putting less than ten cents in the church collection. They have a plate there and there are always lots of dollars, but money is cheap here. I never dreamt of a place where they can earn so much and do so little.

The town is planned very well on the chess board pattern. It sounds stiff and ugly, but it is not because almost every house is painted a different colour and in very pretty colours too. They are detached, built of timber, and quite different in style from each other. Some have gardens in front, some at the back, and some at the sides, so the combined appearance is delightful diversity. All have mosquito-net doors and windows. The flies are in myriads, but the mosquitoes have not bitten me, but some people are smothered in bites. I nearly trod on a snake yesterday—a great thing, about five feet long, black with a brown streak.

Regina is an ideal little city. There is no rowdiness and very little drunkenness or gambling. Mrs. Songhurst says she has only heard of one robbery since she has been here, which is several years. I have only seen about three policemen. There is no workhouse because there are good wages and good work for everyone. There are strict regulations on drunkenness because it was very bad at first. There is only one public house. When a new town arises large enough for a local government, a vote is taken as to whether intoxicating liquor should be sold. If the vote is against, the penalty for selling is very heavy. Of course, they sell it, but they have to be careful.

I attended a wedding in the Anglican Church. A young emigrant had sent for his fiancée to come from England. He had made all the preparations for the wedding, but on her journey, she had fallen in love with a fellow passenger and decided to marry him instead. Financial matters were amicably settled, and the wedding took place as arranged except that the originally intended bridegroom acted as best man. Weddings had a way of going awry. In another case, the girl arrived unexpectedly. The bridegroom took fright and fled. The girl traced him and followed, and so this comedy continued. By the time he reached Duval, where I was then staying, they had seen quite a lot of Saskatchewan and left a trail of bets and laughter behind them.

One day, the Depot Superintendent's wife invited me to see the arrival of the German girl. Two German brothers had adjoining homesteads not far from the town. One had advertised in a Berlin paper for a wife and had paid the girl of his choice her fare. She descended from the train. We watched, from behind curtains, the brothers some distance away. She stood alone stolidly. After a while, the intended husband strolled up and studied her like a buyer at a slave market. Then he turned and walked out of the depot. The girl sat down on her rush-basket hamper. Presently, the other brother strolled up, studied her, picked up her hamper, and nodded to her to follow him.

In a hotel where I once boarded, the bachelor boys used to gather in the parlour and draft advertisements for a wife, just for amusement, and send them to a Saskatoon newspaper for insertion. They spent a hilarious evening reading the replies.

Mrs. Songhurst had noticed my anxiety about getting a post as a teacher. You must go to an agency, she said. I went to the agency, contracted to pay their commission, and obtained a post at Chaplin at a salary of 750 dollars a year.

Teaching in a
One-Room Schoolhouse

G.F. Chipman tells his tale of being a schoolteacher in a one-room schoolhouse on the prairies between 1903 and 1908.[1] He details his experiences finding a suitable teaching position, describes the schoolchildren and their play during recess, and remarks on the boarding home in which he lived during the school year. He describes the rustic conditions of rural teaching and provides a glimpse into the lives led by those children who attended his school.

■

In the frontier settlements of western Canada, the teacher finds many factors entering into his life, which he never heard of when at training school. In the majority of the schools, the teacher, in addition to his pedagogical duties, performs likewise the duty of school janitor, is oft-times the local preacher, and is always the general utility man of the community, dispensing of his supposed, or real, lore to all who may be in need.

The backwoods school, or, as it might more properly be called, the frontier school, and the teacher have been part and parcel of the Canadian national life. The purpose in writing this article is to portray some of the experiences of a teacher in the foreign settlements of western Canada, and it is not the intention to say anything that will belittle these people, who are the backbone of the nation.

I had for several years been teaching in a high school on the Atlantic coast of Canada, where the proud boast of the authorities was that they had the best system and best equipment to be found in the Dominion, and by that they meant any part of the universe. It was while I was engaged in this highly favoured section of Canada that the western fever took a resistless grip on my system, and though I struggled against its influences for two years, I finally yielded and decided to try my fortunes under changed circumstances. With the glowing pictures so vividly portrayed in the sheaves of government literature, which had come to my hands, still floating through my mind, I set out for the lodestone of my desires, nearly four thousand miles towards the setting sun.

I had a friend teaching about twenty miles from Edmonton, the most northerly depot on the Canadian Pacific Railway, and the letters I had received from him were very optimistic on the future of the country. After arriving at Edmonton, I had considerable difficulty in locating him, and it was only after some long drives over rough trails that I finally discovered him in a settlement of Old Country Germans. He was apparently quite happy, though as far as I could see his surroundings were by no means what he had been accustomed to when in the east. He was not expecting me, for though I had told him that I was coming west, I had not stated definitely the time of my departure, and he thought that I had given up all idea of migrating. Greatly surprised, he welcomed me as only one welcomes an old friend when far from home and long absent from the old familiar faces.

I stopped overnight with him and had my first taste of "roughing it" as far as the life of a teacher was concerned. The house, unlike the roomy dwellings of the east, had the upper storey in one room where the family and the visitors slept, a screen being drawn during disrobing and then all thrown into one. This first move was a rather startling innovation, but when we got into the bed and my friend pulled a featherbed over us for a covering, I roared with laughter and woke all the family, for it was late at night when we turned in. I had slept on many different beds, but never had I seen a featherbed used as a covering, though I must admit that it fitted well down over our forms and made a most comfortable and, if clean, would have been a delightful bed.

As my treasury was not in real good shape, I could not spend much time in holidaying, and as there were a number of schools within a radius of twenty-five miles where teachers were wanted, we set out next morning to get the best school possible, with the highest salary. I think my friend took me to some of the most unlikely schools, simply for the sake of giving me all the experience possible. The first section we struck was French, German, and Canadian ratepayers. They had been on the lookout for a teacher but told us that all of those who had made personal applications were too particular and were on the lookout for too long prices to suit them. We soon saw what the matter was, for they wanted a man to not only teach the subjects on the curriculum, but on two afternoons a week to give religious instruction to the children, from both the Catholic and Protestant catechisms. That was enough for me, and without further discussion I jumped into the sleigh and we drove further.

The next place was more promising. I had nearly made up my mind that my search had ended, and only waited to ask after the boarding house. I was shown an old shack, half dugout, where there was a family of only ten already in one room, and the majority of them young children. This was the place where the teacher was supposed to make himself comfortable during the year, and when I came to think the matter over and to consider that I was only going through the world once, I decided that there were better things coming to me if only I could find them, and again we passed on. Finally, after a few more similar experiences, I met with better success and engaged to teach a school not far from my friend's, in a section where the German element predominated but there were a few American and Canadian families to make things easier. The boarding house was not much to look at on the outside, but was all that could be asked for within, and I hoped for a pleasant winter, in which I was not disappointed.

I moved my effects from the depot the next day and made preparations for beginning business on the first day of the week following. The schoolhouse, which, by the way, was also the church, was a log structure eighteen feet wide and twenty-two feet in length, with the chinks between the logs daubed with mud. The

⌃ During the colder times of the year, teachers were expected to keep the classroom warm by lighting the stove before the students arrived in the morning. *Image S73-2639. Courtesy of Provincial Archives of Saskatchewan.*

mud had fallen out in many places, and through these openings the frost of the Alberta winter had free access, and even with all the work we did stoking at the old stove afterwards, the frost was often thick upon the windows all day. The seats were slab benches of primitive style, possessing the minimum of comfort-saving qualities and furnishing splendid opportunities for the children to try out the edge of their knives. The benches were gathered around the old stove, and while the boys and girls near the fire would nearly roast, those far away would be very close to being frostbitten. With a small piece of board on the wall, painted black, the teacher was supposed to have all the equipment necessary for conducting a high-grade western academy.

After lighting the fire on the first morning of school and sweeping out the schoolhouse, which had a superfluous amount of dirt, accumulated during the holidays, I awaited the arrival of the pupils. Usually, in the eastern schools, the children were at the school far ahead of the teacher and sat in all the seats arranged, but I wanted to be on hand to see them arrive. Soon I heard some horses on the run and regular whoops, and coming up the hill were three horses side by side, each putting forth his best efforts to get to the school first, in which they were encouraged by sticks in the hands of their riders. On one horse was two boys, the second carried a boy and a girl, and a third, which was forging ahead, was ridden by two small girls, the smaller one sitting behind with her arms locked around her sister, and apparently as unconcerned as if walking. Another yell announced the fact that they had sighted the new teacher and, pulling up, they quickly dismounted, pulled the bridles from the horses, and sent them home loose. The rest of the pupils soon appeared, some on horseback also, and others, who lived near, walking, and school began.

From the majority of the children, I received nothing beyond a "jah" or a "nein" in response to my first question. They were not timid nor very shy, but didn't like to trust their English as they had been out of practice for some time. This applies mostly to the younger ones, for the older pupils handled the language of their adopted country pretty well. Most of the work at the school was initiating the new pupils into some new paths in the English language, and though I had some boys at school larger than I was, I had, oftentimes, to start them in the first book, and the first rules of arithmetic. When the pupils and teacher were acquainted, the former seemed to want to roam at large over the schoolhouse and sit where the spirit moved them. This was no doubt great fun, and would have kept them all in splendid temper, but it was rather embarrassing to put your hand on a lad when he was most wanted, so I had to remonstrate with them. After a few strong hints, they remained in the places assigned to them and we got along famously.

The girls wore bright-coloured headdresses and had them neatly tied under their chins, making an assemblage of dames, a gay picture. The men wore all kinds of apparel, and some of the clothes they

⌃ School-aged children at their home in Wescott, Alberta, in 1914. *Image NA-2135-4. Courtesy of Glenbow Archives, Archives and Special Collections, University of Calgary.*

would appear out in would cause a great deal of gazing if it were anywhere but in the wilds of the West. When I went to visit the children in their homes, I received the best insight into their peculiar ways and methods. In one of the houses, the proprietor of the ranch had butchered on the afternoon of the day on which I called, and hanging behind the kitchen stove was the carcass of a deceased hog. He had killed it in the kitchen, where the atmosphere was comfortable, and through the night left the pork hanging there to cool. Then, stopping for supper, I was somewhat surprised to see the cake made in the basin that was used to wash in, but when all was ready the food was placed in a big dish in the centre of the table, and each man helped himself. It seemed a queer way to live, but the food was pretty good, and after getting accustomed to the ways, it was one's own fault if he left the house hungry. The log houses of the settlers were very warm, and the rooms were large, so that though there was not often more than three rooms in a house, the family were never far away from each other and often all slept in the same room at night.

Near the houses of all the settlers who had been ten years in the country were small pits, though most of them had begun to fill up, which were the means of obtaining their only means of life when they first came to Canada. This was when there were not many people in the country and the crops had not been good, money was scarce, and the markets were a long piece off, so the most available source of food was the rabbits, which were so plentiful as to be a great nuisance. These pits were cunningly covered with hay, and some turnip or cabbage leaves were thrown in the middle for bait, and when the unsuspecting rabbit went foraging, he fell through the hay and twigs into the pit, where he was hailed with joy on the following morning, and soon his flesh was stewing in the pot for the dinner. Nowadays, when food is plentiful and everybody has plenty, the little quadruped is scorned as food by the majority, but for the good work done by his ancestors in the days of want, he is still tolerated. The old-timers love to tell of the man who ate so much rabbit that the wool started to grow behind his ears, and at last, when he was chased by the dogs, he took to the woods, never being seen or heard of afterwards.

Returning to the school, the legislature of the western provinces has set a splendid example to the other provinces in the matter of school libraries, and it is one of the best things they ever did for their country. In every school, no matter how small, if the teacher is duly qualified and conducts the work properly, a grant especially for the library fund is allowed by the government. This legislation has been the means of placing in every little log schoolhouse a number of splendid books for children, and even some for their elders. I found that the children took a great interest in reading these books and always took them home at night. For those who could not read the books in English, I read to them during half hours on certain afternoons.

The leading sport indulged in by the boys and girls at school was football, and all through the winter, unless the mercury got lower than thirty below zero, they were all out in the road during recess, and kept the pigskin on the merry jump. They knew nothing of the game, and even when I tried to teach them, they preferred to simply kick it and run. The girls were as good players as the boys, and when it came to a heavy body check, the boys usually got the worst of the bargain. Baseball and all the other school games came for a share of attention, but the favourite was always football. It continued to be so all the term and never failed to draw a goodly number of the children.

One night, as three of the boys were going home from school on a long dark trail through the woods on foot, as on fine nights they usually walked home, they were terrified to see following along behind them at a leisurely gait a good-sized bear. It was half a mile to the nearest house, and they went that distance in record time, the bruin keeping the same distance behind them. When they turned in to the house, he ran off into the woods and bothered them no more. It was a long time before any of the children could be induced to take that trail again, either in daylight or in darkness, but finally, when no more bears were seen, they overcame their fright and went home as usual.

At another time a bush fire gave the schoolhouse the closest call it ever had, and but for the good work of the pupils, their academy would have passed into history. The bush at that time grew close around the school, and when the fire was burning a short distance away, it was not thought to be dangerous to the school. Meantime, the wind sprang up and blew the flames towards the building, and then was seen the danger. Rushing to the nearest house, the boys filled some barrels with water and brought them over in a wagon, and by means of a primitive bucket brigade we accomplished what seemed to be impossible. Three of the boys on the roof, some on tables under the eaves, and the rest handing the water made the system complete. For three hours the side and roof of the old log house received a thorough drenching, and when the fire had passed the danger zone, it was a tired but happy group of schoolchildren who wended their way home, all proud of the work they had done and glad that the schoolhouse was saved.

The story of the teaching profession in the West would not be complete without reference to the boarding houses and modes of living. In many of the sections the schools are provided with an extra room at the rear of the house, fitted up for the use of the teacher, and whether male or female they must make themselves comfortable in their bachelor quarters, which are oft-times an improvement on dwellings in the surrounding community. I was fortunate in having gotten into a section where there was a splendid boarding house. It was with an old couple from Kansas, and though the house had only three rooms, and all the company was entertained in my room, yet I never had a better home since I left my own, and I never expect to have one, though I have paid fancy prices, both before and since. Lying in bed with the woods all around, and being lulled to sleep by the howling, or I prefer to call it the singing, of the coyotes and the dismal hoot of the owls, is a pleasure that is denied those who are compelled to live in more civilized parts of the country.

The westerners set a splendid example to easterners in the matter of salaries. They expect a man to do the work and also expect to pay him enough to live on, and in comparison to the salary in a similar school in the East, the pay is certainly princely. It is still going up, and before long the profession will be able to hold the best who may enter into its arduous duties.

The teacher in the West has some distinct advantages over his friend in the East, being known far and wide as the teacher, and invited to every function for miles around. They all keep cayuses (i.e., ponies) and are independent in travelling, so that in itself more than offsets many of the other inconveniences. These schools will exist in Canada as long as the immigration continues, which will be for many, many years yet to come, and the teacher will be a necessary part of the frontier life for the same time.

Afterthoughts

The individual stories that are set out above do not encompass all of the situations that homesteaders experienced. Rather, they give a snapshot of the lives of those who travelled to, and lived on, the western prairies. By reading their stories, we gain insight into the problems and challenges that many of them faced, whether they were travelling by ship, train, or horse and wagon; building their homes; dealing with the harshness of the climate or the ruggedness of the terrain. Their encounters with others who were also homesteading, their friendship and co-operative spirit, are also evident in the stories, and this helps illustrate how companionship was essential to prairie living.

Moving to a region that offered few or no amenities meant that individuals were reliant on themselves and their families, including their children, to eke out a living. All laboured on the homestead; all had chores to undertake every day in order for the family to meet the homestead requirements and obtain the patent to their land. There was a gendered division of labour, with mothers being primarily responsible for undertaking the domestic chores within the household. Washing clothes, making beds, cooking three meals a day, churning butter, sewing clothes, quilting blankets, beating rugs, canning and preserving food, weeding gardens, and feeding small farm animals and chickens were all under the purview of the farm wife. Fathers, on the other hand, were expected to handle the more labour-intensive duties in the fields, clearing the land of trees and rocks, ploughing, seeding, and harvesting. They also worked with the large farm animals, such as horses, oxen, and cattle. They cut reams of firewood for the cookstove; built barns, granaries, and shelters as needed; and took care of the household accounts. Children, as soon as they were able, were assisting in the garden or fields, pulling weeds and gathering rocks, and performing simple domestic tasks such as washing dishes or sweeping the floors. As children aged, they assumed more difficult tasks around the farmyard and in the farmhouse, with both boys and girls, by the age of fourteen, handling the same amount of labour as their parents. Whether homesteaders and their families were undertaking domestic chores within the home or performing fieldwork, the daily labour was never-ending. Each day, and with each passing season, farm labour, in all its various forms, had to be accomplished in order for the family to survive.

While many homesteaders in their memoirs discussed the amount of work that was involved in setting up a homestead, others who settled on the prairies commented on the harshness of the climate, particularly the viciousness of the long winter months. Blizzards and freezing temperatures were a threat to humans and animals alike if preparations had not been made. Being caught in storms, trying desperately to shield themselves from the elements, or relying on their horses to pull them through to safety were memories imprinted on the minds of those homesteaders who had experienced such traumatic situations. Cyclones also posed hazards to the homesteaders. The powerful force of the shrieking winds destroyed their homes and barns in seconds and threatened the lives of those who could not find, or did not have the time to find, shelter.

Prairie fires were another constant menace. At any time during the warm months of the year, fires might be racing across the fields towards the homesteading family. Feelings of great fear and anxiety were expressed by those who faced this danger, and stories were told of families fighting this threat to their lives and livelihood. Even when their efforts to fight the fire were successful, the destruction of crops, and the death of farm animals and family members or friends, often followed in the path of those fires.

Along with these tales of work and hardship, there were also homesteaders who expressed their delight with their surroundings. They conveyed the joy and wonder they felt when viewing the vast open spaces of the prairies, the beauty of the aurora borealis, the friendliness of the wild animals, and the dancing of the prairie chickens in the spring. Some people enjoyed journeying from one place to another while they searched for work (and eventually found employment in a variety of odd jobs), while others recounted building up businesses and moving products by scow on the North Saskatchewan River. Still others became schoolteachers in one-room schoolhouses, while others ventured west in the hope of becoming wives and husbands and raising a family.

For many, however, the primary draw to the prairies was the offer of free land: 160 acres for a ten-dollar registration fee. The opportunity to own their own land was a once-in-a-lifetime event. Regardless of the challenges that they had to endure, many people who came to the western prairies looked forward to the future. They felt that homesteading was a chance to improve not only their own lives, but also the lives of future generations of their family. They worked hard to accomplish this task that they had set for themselves, and in the end, many were successful and gained title to their land.

As readers can see from the various stories in this collection, each homesteader's experiences were unique, but at the same time, the immigrants and migrants who came west were all part of a distinctive era that brought them together. People of different nationalities, different cultures, and different economic and political backgrounds all made their way to Alberta, Saskatchewan, and Manitoba. They became part of a cohesive whole, all with the purpose and intent of creating homes and prosperous communities on the prairies.

Their drive and ambition, and their hopes for the future, are likely what encouraged them to write their memoirs before they passed. They knew that they were part of an exceptional time in Canadian history, a time of exhilaration, excitement, adventure, and anticipation that will never again be experienced by anyone.

With these memoirs, readers can learn about the homesteading era through the eyes of the homesteaders themselves. Each person and each family had their own narrative, and they offer their personal perspectives about homesteading using their own words and thoughts. Their stories are important, as their feelings, behaviours, thoughts, and actions help personalize the historical facts that have been written about the era. In addition, these stories highlight what was important to those who lived during that time. As we have read, some stories are humorous and induce laughter, while others are serious and troubling, evoking sympathy and sadness. A gamut of situations were experienced by the men, women, and children who homesteaded across the western prairies, and as we learn more about these individuals, we come to admire and appreciate their courage, persistence, and fortitude. They forged a new life for themselves, and through their hard work and belief in the future, they helped to ensure the future prosperity of not only their own families but also the province in which they lived—the province they called home.

∨ A homesteading family standing proudly in front of their home in the Mankota district of Saskatchewan in the early 1900s. *Image R-A492-1. Courtesy of Provincial Archives of Saskatchewan.*

Acknowledgements

I would like to thank my friends and family members who have been so supportive of my research efforts over the past thirty years. In particular, I would like to express my appreciation to my MacEwan University colleagues, and to the staff at the archives located in Edmonton, Calgary, Lethbridge, Saskatoon, Regina, and Winnipeg. I would also like to thank those from Heritage House Publishing who helped bring this book to fruition including Lara Kordic, Nandini Thaker, Audrey McClellan, Monica Miller, Kimiko Fraser, Martin Gavin, and Colin Parks. Thanks are also extended to my mother, MaryEtta Rollings—a homesteader's granddaughter—for her suggestions and comments, and to David Shiers and Christina Magnusson for their ongoing encouragement.

Endnotes

Preface

[1] A revision to the *Dominion Lands Act* in 1876 provided an opportunity for those women who could prove that they were heads of their own households and responsible for dependents. If they fit into this category, they could register for homestead land.

[2] For details on the *Dominion Lands Act,* see K.M. Lambrecht, *The Administration of Dominion Lands, 1870–1930* (Regina: Canadian Plains Research Center, 1991).

[3] For more information on the push and pull movements to the western prairies, see Sandra Rollings-Magnusson, "Steerage, Cattle Cars and Red River Carts: Travelling to the Canadian Western Prairies to Homestead, 1876–1914," *Journal of Family History* 39, no. 2 (2014): 140–74.

[4] For more on the 1911 census see the Library and Archives Canada website: https://www.bac-lac.gc.ca/eng/census/1911/Pages/about-census.aspx.

[5] "The Homestead Act of 1862," US National Archives and Records Administration website, accessed online May 1, 2015, http://www.archives.gov/education/lessons/homestead-act/.

[6] Jean Bruce, *The Last Best West* (Toronto: Fitzhenry and Whiteside, 2000).

[7] See Sandra Rollings-Magnusson, "Flax Seed, Goose Grease, and Gun Powder: Medical Practices by Women Homesteaders in Saskatchewan (1882–1914)," *Journal of Family History* 33, no. 4 (2008): 388–410.

[8] C.E. Kieper Diary, Accession No. A 75, Provincial Archives of Saskatchewan (PAS).

Tossed into the Scuppers

[1] Emily Wright Millar's memoir "Beyond the Sunset," Accession No. A210, PAS.

The City Paved with Gold

[1] Herman Collingwood Memoirs, Accession No. R77-86, PAS.

[2] The Boer War (actually the Second Boer War) between British forces and two Boer states in southern Africa (the South African Republic and the Orange Free State) occurred between 1899 and 1902. The First Boer War took place from 1880 to 1881. Boers were white descendants of Dutch settlers in the area. "Boer" means "farmer" in Dutch and Afrikaans, the language of the white South Africans.

[3] Wilfrid Laurier was the prime minister of Canada from 1896 to 1911, and as such had a direct hand in the homesteading process on the western prairies.

[4] During Herman's time, the phrase "picked up" meant "met."

[5] Bully beef is made of minced corned beef and gelatin.

[6] The parkland area of the province, now known as Aspen Parkland, was a desirable one. "This ecoregion extends in a broad arc from southwestern Manitoba, northwestward through Saskatchewan to its northern apex in central Alberta. The parkland is considered transitional between the boreal forest to the north and the grasslands to the south. The climate is marked by short, warm summers and long, cold winters with continuous snow cover . . . The ecoregion also provides a major breeding habitat for waterfowl and includes habitat for white-tailed deer, coyote, snowshoe hare, cottontail, red fox, northern pocket gopher, Franklin's ground squirrel, and bird species like sharp-tailed grouse and black-billed magpie. Because of its favourable climate and fertile, warm black soils, this ecoregion represents some of the most productive agricultural land in the Prairies . . . Major communities include Red Deer, Edmonton, Lloydminster, North Battleford, Humboldt, Yorkton, and Brandon." From "Ecoregions of Saskatchewan," Virtual Herbarium, University of Saskatchewan, biolwww.usask.ca/rareplants_sk/root/htm/en/researcher/4_ecoreg.php.

The Flyer

[1] Pioneer Questionnaire, SX2-1086, PAS.

Green Englishmen Were Not Wanted

[1] Pioneer Questionnaire, SX2-2308, PAS.

[2] In 1907, the homestead duties included breaking and cropping ten acres in the first year and fifteen acres in both the second and third years, so that forty acres were cultivated in total. This was according to a revision in the *Dominion Lands Act*. (See S.C. 1891 54-55 Victoria c. 24 ss. 2, 3, 4).

Keeping the Home Fires Burning

[1] C.E. Kieper Diary, Accession No. A 75, PAS.

Life Here Was Not Like in Denmark

[1] Christen Anders Christensen's memoir "As I Remember," Accession No. 76.63 SE, Provincial Archives of Alberta (PAA).

Building a Bloc Settlement

[1] Leopold Lippert's memoir "The Story of Leopold Lippert," Accession No. 81.342 SE, PAA.

True Grit

[1] Cecilia Hryzak Kissel's memoir "Hardships they Faced," Accession No. SA 474, PAS.

[2] McCreary was most likely an agent with the Dominion Lands Office.

[3] Information on Frank Pedley is from "Key People in Land Demand, Consent, Acquisition," in Peggy Martin-McGuire, *First Nation Land Surrenders on the Prairies, 1896-1911* (Ottawa: Indian Claims Commission, 1998), 494, https://publications.gc.ca/collections/collection_2017/trp-sct/RC31-93-1998-9-eng.pdf

Lost Luggage

[1] Annie Condon's memoir "Northern Lights: A Story of Pioneer Days in Saskatchewan," Accession No. A535, PAS.

[2] A large number of men from Ontario, Quebec, and the Maritimes would travel by train to the western prairies to help with threshing the wheat fields every fall. This was seen as an opportunity for temporary/seasonal employment, but it also gave the men a chance to experience western living and perhaps register for a homestead themselves. See John Thompson, "Bringing in the Sheaves: The Harvest Excursionists of 1908," *Canadian Historical Review* 59, no. 4 (1978): 467–89.

[3] There was no explanation in the file as to why the land was purchased. It could be that Annie Condon's husband purchased homestead land from the Dominion Lands Office at three dollars an acre, bought it from another farmer who had already proved and obtained the title to the land, or he could have purchased a quarter-section from the CPR.

[4] A guimpe is a high-necked blouse.

[5] Otherwise known as mountain ash.

Travelling in a Cattle Car

[1] Mrs. Minnie Taphorn Memoir, Accession No. A 81, PAS.

The Wedding Trip

[1] Mrs. Edna Banks's memoir "Swift Flowing," Accession No. R-E2912, PAS.

[2] As mentioned in the Preface, after a homesteader had received his patent for the original homestead, he was entitled to a pre-emption. He had to pay the federal government for this additional quarter-section at an amount set by the government. If the homesteader did not take advantage of this opportunity within two years after the patent for the original homestead was received, the opportunity was forfeited and the land was then reopened for homestead entry to others (SC 1906 c 55, s 127). It should also be noted that pre-emptions were only offered by the federal government for certain periods of time between 1871 and 1890 and 1908 to 1918. See Kirk Lambrecht, *The Administration of Dominion Lands, 1870–1930* (Regina: Canadian Plains Research Center, 1991).

[3] Mackinaw coats were made of a heavy water-repellant material.

Horse Thieves

[1] History of the Phillips Family, Accession No. 67.99 SE, PAA.

Travelling by Scow to Lloydminster

[1] Madge Isabel Strong's memoir "Our Family Returns to Canada," Accession No. 68.93/1.5, PAA.

[2] Jasper is mentioned in the biblical book of Revelations, chapter 21, in a description of the heavenly city of God, where jasper is used in the walls and the foundation, and the city itself is described as having the brilliance of jasper.

Daily Living

[1] Sylvia Mitchell's memoir "Pioneering in Saskatchewan," Accession No. R-E94, PAS.

Never a Dull Moment

[1] Evelyn Slater McLeod's memoir "Restless Pioneers," Accession No. 77.39, PAA.

Flour Sacks, Mice, and Rain

[1] Autobiography of Gladys Marie Kennedy, Accession No. 86-459 SE, PAA.

Cattle Ranching

[1] William Colby Reesor memoir, Accession No. 77.57SE, PAA.

The Homesteader and the Teacher

[1] Pioneer Questionnaires SX2-416, PAS.

The West Is No Place for a Loafer or a Kicker

[1] Mabel (Wilson) Hawthorne's memoir "My Reminiscence of Fifty Years on the Saskatchewan Prairie," Accession No. RE 2991, PAS.

[2] The Princess Pats are the Princess Patricia's Canadian Light Infantry, formed in 1914 at the outbreak of the First World War. It was named for the daughter of the Governor General at the time.

All Gone into the Dust of Time

[1] Joan S. Phelps memoir "Legacy of Love," Accession No. A 323, PAS.

The Great Blast of a Cyclone

[1] Pioneer Questionnaire SX2-841, PAS.

[2] A 9.2 refers to a German howitzer, an artillery piece with a high trajectory.

The Fury of the Wind and Blinding Snow

[1] Pioneer Questionnaire SX2-1086, PAS.

[2] In an English nursery rhyme written in the early 1800s, Old Mother Hubbard went to the cupboard but found it was so bare there wasn't even a bone available for the dog. (https://allnurseryrhymes.com/old-mother-hubbard/)

[3] The Bessborough is a luxury hotel built in Saskatoon, Saskatchewan, in the 1920s by the CPR.

Nipper Saved our Lives

[1] Pioneer Questionnaire SX2-544, PAS.

Lack of Medical Help

[1] Interview with R.R. Knight, Accession No. C 60, PAS.

Prairie Fire and Desolation

[1] Dorothy Gush's memoir "Prairie Years from 1905 to 1909," Accession No. A266, PAS.

Many Happy Incidences

[1] Delia Bigelow Woolf, Oral History Program, Accession No. 74-4 74/4-6, PAA.

[2] Fistulous withers is caused by an infected bursa in the area of the withers—the highest point of the horse's back, above the shoulders and at the base of the neck. A horse suffering from such an ailment will experience swelling between the shoulders and chronic pain.

Adventure Is What I Wanted and It Is What I Got

[1] Pioneer Questionnaire SX2-843, PAS.

[2] A buckeye is a light wagon drawn by one horse.

A Little Girl's Thoughts

[1] Pioneer Questionnaire SX2-1114, PAS.

Eliza Jane (Brown) Wilson's Daily Journal

[1] Eliza Jane (Brown) Wilson Daily Journal, Accession No. A-W749, Glenbow Archives.

The Sod Shack

[1] James Rugg Reminiscences, Accession No. A100, PAS.

Freedom of the Wild

[1] Berkner Family Reminiscences, Accession No. A454, PAS.

Appreciation for Her Mother

[1] Olive Lockhart Memoirs, Accession No. R82-372, PAS.

Grace to the Haggis

[1] Pioneer Questionnaire SX2-884, PAS.

A Dirty Deal

[1] Gordon Wolseley Stewart memoirs, Accession No. 82-57, PAS.

[2] Dockage would be deducted if there were too many weed seeds mixed in with the grain, if the grain was not ripe enough, or if it was not dry enough. In such cases, the grain would be deemed to be of lesser quality by the elevator operator. In other words, the quality of the grain and the amount paid was at the operator's sole discretion.

The People of Regina

[1] Mrs. W.T. Billings memoir "An English School Marm in Saskatchewan," Accession No. A160, PAS.

Teaching in a One-Room Schoolhouse

[1] G.F. Chipman Papers, Accession No. 69.162/1-100, PAA.

Bibliography

Abbreviations:

PAA Provincial Archives of Alberta, Edmonton, Alberta.

PAS Provincial Archives of Saskatchewan, Saskatoon and Regina, Saskatchewan.

PRIMARY SOURCES – ARCHIVAL

Allan, John M. (1950–56). Pioneer Questionnaire SX2-884, PAS.

Banks, Mrs. Edna. (n.d.) Memoir. "Swift Flowing," Accession No. R-E2912, PAS.

Berkner Family. (n.d.) Reminiscences, Accession No. A454, PAS.

Billing, Mrs. W.T. (n.d.) Memoir. "An English School Marm in Saskatchewan," Accession No. A 160, PAS.

Brown, Eliza Jane. (1901). Daily Journal. Accession No. A-W749, Glenbow Archives.

Cardwell, Phyllis I. (1950–56). Pioneer Questionnaire SX2-1114, PAS.

Chipman, G.F. (n.d.) Memoir. Accession No. 69.162/1-100, PAA.

Christensen, Christen Anders. (n.d.) Memoir. "As I Remember," Accession No. 76.63 SE, PAA.

Collingwood, Herman. (n.d.) Memoir. "My Life History from 1904 to 1970 in Saskatchewan," Accession No. R77-86, PAS.

Condon, Annie. (n.d.) Memoir. "Northern Lights: A Story of Pioneer Days in Saskatchewan," Accession No. A535, PAS.

Elderton, Albert E. (1950–56). Pioneer Questionnaire, SX2-1086, PAS.

Gudmundson, G.F. (1950–56). Pioneer Questionnaire SX2-841, PAS.

Gush, Dorothy. (1968). Memoir. "Prairie Years from 1905 to 1909," Accession No. A266, PAS.

Hammerschmidt, Joseph. (1950–56), Pioneer Questionnaire SX2-843, PAS.

Hawthorne, Mabel (Wilson). (n.d.) Memoir. "My Reminiscence of Fifty Years on the Saskatchewan Prairie," Accession No. RE 2991, PAS.

Kennedy, Gladys M. (1970). Autobiography. Accession No. 86-459 SE, PAA.

Kieper, Charles.E. (1954). Diary. Accession No. A 75, PAS.

Kissel, Cecilia Hryzak. (n.d.) Memoir. "Hardships they Faced," Accession No. SA 474, PAS.

Knight, R.R. (1964). Interview. Accession No. C 60, PAS.

Lippert, Leopold. (n.d.) Memoir. "The Story of Leopold Lippert," Accession No. 81.342 SE, PAA.

Lockhart, Olive. (n.d.) Memoir. Accession No. R82-372, PAS.

McLeod, Evelyn Slater (1977). Memoir. "Restless Pioneers," Accession No. 77.39, PAA.

Mitchell, Sylvia. (1976). Memoir. "Pioneering in Saskatchewan," Accession No. R-E94, PAS.

Phelps, Joan S. (1979). Memoir. "Legacy of Love," Accession No. A 323, PAS.

Phillips, Charles P. (1967). Memoir. History of the Phillips Family. Accession No. 67.99 SE, PAA.

Purdy, Lena May. (1950–56). Pioneer Questionnaire SX2-416, PAS.

Reesor, William Colby. (n.d.) Memoir. Accession No. 77.57SE, PAA.

Robinson, W. (1950–56). Pioneer Questionnaire, SX2-2308, PAS.

Rugg, James. (1961). Reminiscences, Accession No. A100, PAS.

Stewart, Gordon W. (n.d.) Memoirs, Accession No. 82-57, PAS.

Strong, Madge Isabel. (n.d.) Memoir. "Our Family Returns to Canada," Accession No. 68.93/1.5, PAA.

Taphorn, Minnie. (n.d.). Memoir. Accession No. A 81, PAS.

Wood, Robert G. (1950–56). Pioneer Questionnaire SX2-544, PAS.

Woolf, Delia Bigelow. (1974). Interview. Accession No. 74-4 74/4-6, PAA.

Wright Millar, Emily. (1976). Memoir. "Beyond the Sunset," Accession No. A210, PAS.

PRIMARY SOURCES—GOVERNMENT

Census of Canada, 1911. Library and Archives Canada. June 20, 2019. https://www.bac-lac.gc.ca/eng/census/1911/Pages/about-census.aspx.

Dominion Lands Act, 1872 (Canada).

The Homestead Act of 1862. US National Archives and Records Administration. May 1, 2015. http://www.archives.gov/ education/lessons/homestead-act/

SECONDARY SOURCES

Bruce, Jean. *The Last Best West.* Toronto: Fitzhenry and Whiteside, 2000.

Bryant, William Cullen. *The Prairies.* Poetry Foundation. June 20, 2019. https://www.poetryfoundation.org/poems/55341/the-prairies.

Ecoregions of Saskatchewan. Virtual Herbarium, University of Saskatchewan. June 1, 2016. http://www.usask.ca/biology/rare-plants_sk/root/htm/en/researcher/4_ecoreg.php.

Lambrecht, Kirk M. The Administration of Dominion Lands, 1870–1930. Regina: Canadian Plains Research Center, 1991.

Martin-McGuire, Peggy. "Key People in Land Demand, Consent, Acquisition." In *First Nation Land Surrenders on the Prairies, 1896–1911*. Ottawa: Indian Claims Commission, 1998. https://publications.gc.ca/collections/collection_2017/trp-sct/RC31-93-1998-9-eng.pdf.

Old Mother Hubbard. All Nursery Rhymes. June 1, 2019. (https://all-nurseryrhymes.com/old-mother-hubbard/)

Rollings-Magnusson, Sandra. "Flax Seed, Goose Grease, and Gun Powder: Medical Practices by Women Homesteaders in Saskatchewan, 1882–1914." *Journal of Family History* 33, no. 4 (2008): 388–410.

———. "Steerage, Cattle Cars and Red River Carts: Travelling to the Canadian Western Prairies to Homestead, 1876–1914." *Journal of Family History* 39, no. 2 (2014): 140–74.

Thompson, John. "Bringing in the Sheaves: The Harvest Excursionists of 1908." *Canadian Historical Review* 59, no. 4 (1978): 467–89.

Index

crops
berries, 98, 124, 174–75, 208
CPR and, 215–22
drought and, 122
flax, 219–20
vegetables, 54, 98, 194
wheat, 52, 124, 127–31, 219, 221
Cumberland, Dr., 140
cyclones, 98, 137–41, 198, 223–24

Danes, 33–38
Dauphin, 57
Davies, Johanna, 134, 135
Davies, Mary Ellen "Peggy," 134–35
Davies, Thomas, 133–35
Day, Daniel, 104
Day, Dr. Arthur, 104
democrat (carriage), 54, 65, 96, 159, 162
DeWolfe, Esther, 106
diptheria, 29
disease and illnesses, xiii, 22, 29, 37, 40, 41, 42–43, 44, 94, 104, 106, 151–52
    See also doctors
dockage, 215, 218, 219, 220–21
doctors, 13, 30, 44, 94, 99, 104, 140, 141, 157–60, 184
    See also accidents and injuries; disease and illnesses
Dominion Lands Office, 65, 66–67
dowsing, 98, 104
Draheim, Augusta, 27, 29–30
droughts, 122, 210
Ducholm family, 37
ducks, 17, 96, 155, 193, 199, 202, 203, 206, 209, 210
"Duke of Argyll," 212–13
Duval, 227

Edmonton, 40, 48, 53, 86, 87
Edson Trail, 110
Elderton, Albert E. "Bert," 19–20, 143–46
Elfros, 140, 141
Elstow, 198
English settlers, 1–11, 21–25, 34, 159, 161–69, 197–200, 223–28

fires, 91, 92–94, 96–98, 163–65, 168–69, 182, 184, 185, 193, 199, 208, 236, 240
First Nations, 90, 151

Muenster, 60
muskrats, 203

Nantglyn, 133
North Battleford, 156, 157, 159
North Saskatchewan River, 86, 87–91
North West Mounted Police, 30, 48, 91, 189, 227
North-West Territories, 16, 18, 31, 52
Norwegians, 12

oxen
    caring for, 164, 168
    as draft animals, 25, 31, 43, 46, 96, 127, 162, 165, 184, 185
    vs. horses, 53, 163

Palson, Dr., 140, 141
Patagonia, 134
Pedley, Frank, 49
pets, 31, 100, 101, 111, 208
Phelps, Joan S., 133–35
Phillips, Charles Jr., 79–84
Phillips, Charles Sr., 79–84
Phillips, Glen, 79
pigs, 17, 122, 124, 190, 199–200, 209, 210, 213–14, 234
police, 30, 48, 91, 189, 227
Port Arthur, 55
Portage la Prairie, 57
poultry, 185, 199, 207, 210, 226
prices, 226
Prickly Pear Canyon, 83
Purdue, Sid, 161
Purdy, Herb, 121
Purdy, Lena May, 121–24
Purdy, Russel, 121, 123, 124
Purdy, Walter, 122, 123
Purdy, Will, 121, 122, 124

Qu'Appelle, 17, 18, 134
Quill Lake, 53–54

rabbits, 42, 43, 44–45, 96, 100, 163, 199, 208, 210, 235
railways
    accidents, 19–20, 56

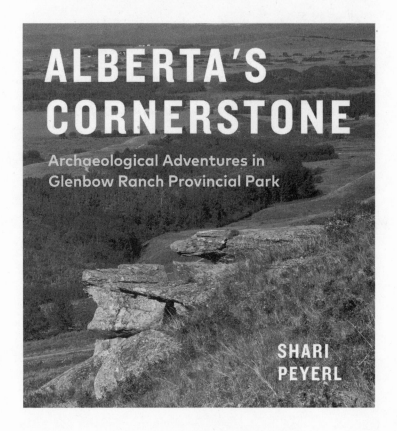

Alberta's Cornerstone

Archaeological Adventures in Glenbow Ranch Provincial Park

Shari Peyerl

ISBN 978-1-77203-391-5 (paperback)
ISBN 978-1-77203-392-2 (ebook)

*The fascinating exploration of a vanished settlement
in Glenbow Ranch Provincial Park, told within
the framework of an archaeologist's memoir.*